HELLO, DARLING!
WANT TO
PICK UP A
PENGUIN?

SEXUAL TRIVIA

Sarah Curtis

Cartoons by Tom Johnston

WARD LOCK LIMITED · LONDON

First published in Great Britain in 1986
by Ward Lock Limited, 8 Clifford Street
London W1X 1RB, an Egmont Company

Text set in Times New Roman
by Cheney & Sons Ltd., Banbury
Printed and bound in Glasgow by
William Collins

British Library Cataloguing in Publication Data
Curtis, Sarah
Sexual trivia.
1. Sex—Anecdotes, facetiae, satire, etc.
i. Title
306.7'0207 HQ23

ISBN 0-7063-6496-1 Paperback
ISBN 0-7063-6571-2 Cased

Foreplay

When it comes to sex we are a nation of incurable informa-niacs. Who does what to whom – and more importantly how often – preoccupies a great chunk of our lives. As obsessions go it is all quite indecently below the belt. Entire industries flourish on our fascination with the simplest pleasure which gives rise to the greatest anxiety – and we still show no sign of giving it up!

Sexual Trivia charts the facts, the figures, the frustration and the fun. If it teaches you nothing more about sex, you will at least discover why big-breasted women are a danger to aircraft, how 300 stud bunnies came to drop dead doing what comes naturally, and when 10,000 armed gays swept through Europe.

Also included are the results of the strangest sex surveys. But remember, as one sexologist says, it is the subject every-one lies most about. Sex can bring out the best – and worst in us. I always remember the story of the archbishop who flew to New York and gave an airport press conference on landing. As questions were fired from all sides, a reporter barked: 'What do you think about the brothels on the East Side?' Wary of being misquoted the archbishop cautiously asked: 'Are there any?' Two hours later the first editions splashed: ARCHBISHOP'S FIRST QUESTION – ARE THERE ANY BROTHELS ON THE EAST SIDE?

We can't believe everything we read, but on the subject of sex even the wildest stories are probably true.

SARAH CURTIS

N

Influential Men whose Sexual Organs are preserved

•*Rasputin*
The bearded mystic, womanizer and confidante of the Tsar met a very nasty end. He was murdered by poison, shooting and stabbing, before his body was finally flung into a freezing St Petersburg river. Rasputin was allegedly castrated during the fatal attack. His penis was retrieved and kept by one of his many lovers. In 1968 the old lady was reported to be living in Paris where she kept the shrivelled memento in a wooden box on top of a bedroom cupboard (well, where would *you* keep a fifty-year-old sexual organ?). Patte Barham, Rasputin's biographer, reported that 'it looked like a blackened, overripe banana, about a foot long, and resting on a velvet cloth.'

•*Napoleon Bonaparte*
As if Bonaparte had not been maligned enough, the final ignominy came 150 years after his death when his preserved penis failed to fetch reserve price when it came up for auction at Christie's. The catalogue described the inch-long (2.5 cm) artefact as 'a small, dried-up object.' A later attempt to sell it in a mail-order catalogue also found no takers. Its final resting place was in the collection of an American urologist, who purchased it for around £2,500.

•*Jesus Christ*
A religious relic, known as the Holy Prepuce, is claimed to be the foreskin of Jesus Christ. Unfortunately it can no longer be exposed to the faithful who flocked to see it in the medieval village of Calcata, north of Rome. The Holy foreskin said to date from Christ's circumcision in the Temple, was stolen in 1984 from a wardrobe shelf in the home of parish priest Don Dario Magnoni. The *Sunday Times* quoted the local *carabinieri* as saying: 'The object was old, in bad condition – small too. It is unlikely to be found.'

Books with Unintentionally Risqué Titles

Making It In Leather (David & Charles, 1973)
Penetrating Wagner's Ring (Da Capo, 1978)
Women On The Job (Lexington Books, 1979)
The Gay Boys Of Old Yale (Hunter, 1869)
The Big Problem Of Small Organs (Kitley, 1966)
How To Love Every Minute of Your Life (Prentice-Hall, 1978)

Unusual Methods of Contraception

• *The Traffic-light Bra*
A device tested at Glasgow Infirmary which detects changes in body temperature during ovulation. The bra – to be worn for nine days at the usual time of ovulation – turns green if it is safe to make love, and red if the outlook is risky. Instructions for the colour-blind are not included.

• *Elephant Dung*
Popular among Persians in the tenth century. Clearly enthused by the Egyptian penchant for crocodile dung pessaries, the Persian writer Rhazes recommended an improved method using rolled-up balls of elephant dung. Presumably the biggest problem faced by passionate Persians was first to catch the elephant.

• *Sneezing*
Soranos, a Roman doctor who specialized in gynaecological problems, gave much thought to the question of contraception. The best method, he concluded, was for the woman to hold her breath when her partner ejaculated, and afterwards to sneeze violently. It certainly makes a change from sharing a cigarette.

BLOW-UP
ELEPHANT

• *Blackmail*
Medical centres on the balmy Indonesian island of Bali display maps indicating which families do not use contraceptives. The resulting social stigma sends guilty couples scurrying to the family planning clinic.

• *Coca-Cola*
Scientists at Harvard Medical School discovered that Coke was being used as a douche by women in developing countries. Tests found that it had a 91 per cent success rate in killing sperm. New formula Coke, however, was only 42 per cent successful, but Diet Coke was found to be 100 per cent effective. For those inclined to try, it cannot be recommended as a birth control method as sperm can fertilize before you have time to reach for a six-pack. As a Coca-Cola spokesman said: 'We make no claims in this direction.'

• *Superglue*
The World Health Organization has carried out long-term tests in Lancashire, England, on a method of sealing the Fallopian tube with a newly-developed type of superglue. If successful, it will prevent eggs escaping to the womb. If not, it must have 1,001 household uses.

Brief Encounter

In 1980, Julie Barlow, an anthropology student, was waiting to use a Chicago public telephone when a man stepped in front of her and suddenly exposed himself. 'What do you think of that, then?' he leered. Ms Barlow squinted at the offending member: 'It looks like a cock to me,' she said cooly. 'Only smaller.'

Imaginative Names for Male Genitals in Current Usage

Almond rock candy
Bald-headed hermit
Beard-splitter
Dead rabbit
Ferret
Ice-cream machine
Jewish complaint
Kidney wiper
Lung disturber
Marquis of Lorne
Pink oboe
Pork dagger
Whirligigs

Unusual Sexual Experiences of Famous Poets

•*Lord Byron* had sex with his nanny at the age of nine. Other conquests included schoolboy chums at Harrow, a conservatively-estimated 300 women, and his married half-sister, Augusta Leigh.

•*Algernon Swinburne* had a well-documented taste for flagellation. He is also said to have had sexual relations with a pet monkey. No records of the ape's reaction to these encounters exist, however.

•*Rainer Maria Rilke's* mother desperately wanted a girl. By way of compensation the poet spent a confused boyhood wearing dresses and answering to the name of Sophie.

Six Creatures Prone to Gay Behaviour

Pigeons
Baboons
Geese
Ten-spined sticklebacks
Dolphins
Snails

Passion Killers

Monsieur Philippe Dubois and his new bride travelled to the idyllic island of Reunion in the Indian Ocean for a June honeymoon in 1977. In the tropical moonlight Monsieur Dubois, on a romantic stroll with his wife, playfully vaulted the garden fence surrounding their rented bungalow. His body was later discovered in the crater of an extremely deep volcano.

In 1981 German newspapers reported the case of a woman who believed she could stimulate her husband by frightening him. Her theory was that the sudden rush of adrenalin made him do unpredictable things. This indeed proved to be tragically true. When she heard her husband return from work one evening, hungry for love, she hid in a cupboard and leapt out screaming. The unfortunate fellow turned and fled, tripped over a carpet and plunged headlong through an upstairs window.

Imaginative Names for Female Genitals in Current Usage

Eve's custom house
Cat with its throat cut
Growl and grunt (rhyming slang)
Hair pie
Jerusalem artichoke
Little man in the boat
Mark of the beast
Where the monkey sleeps
YMCA

Escape Fever

Love was never put more to the test than when Yugoslavian Oscar Morand courted his girl-friend Marie Glesk who lived across the Iron Curtain in Hungary. Every time they had a date Oscar had to crawl commando-style through a minefield at night. One evening, to his great relief, Marie agreed to crawl back with him and get married.

Shop-girl Trena Rowland rounded off a romantic evening with her boy-friend by being questioned by sheriff's deputies. As the couple kissed on her sofa in Harrison, Michigan, Miss Rowland's passion became uncontrollable, and she accidentally bit off his tongue. Police arrived at the house to find the victim shocked and speechless with a 2in (5cm) piece of the evidence lying on the carpet.

When the last customer had gone home from San Francisco's Condor Club, the barman and the topless cabaret dancer exchanged a look of understanding. They climbed onto the flat top of the white grand piano and made love passionately. Unfortunately their abandon shook the instrument so vigorously that they triggered a hydraulic mechanism which raised the piano to the roof of the building. Sixteen-stone (101kg) Jimmy 'The Beard' Ferrozzo was found the next morning crushed to death between his nude partner and the ceiling. The dancer, pinned beneath him, was amazingly unhurt and too drunk to even recall climbing onto the piano.

In 1983 the Kenya News Agency reported the strange case of two lovers who had to be taken to Nairobi hospital for medical treatment after a witch doctor put a curse on them. The magician, hired by the women's cuckolded husband, proved extremely efficient. The lovers became stuck together when they made love. Neighbours who heard their scream were unable to separate them. Police had to carry the couple, still joined together, on a stretcher to hospital to be prised apart by doctors.

More than 300 expensive stud rabbits died of heat-stroke while energetically mating when midday temperatures on their Barcelona farm rose to 46°C (115°F).

The prospect of a night of love under the stars proved too much for a London couple to resist. They climbed onto the roof of a supermarket in a shopping mall and, in the course of

MICK!
YOU SHOULDN'T PRACTISE KISSING WITH A GROW-BAG!
GRASS SEED
GROW BAG

their exertions, rolled through a skylight, plunging 15 feet (4.5m) onto a grocery display. The resounding crash triggered the store's burglar alarms and brought police racing to the scene to find the lovers dazed, but unhurt.

How the Stars Lost Their Virginity

Mick Jagger – in a garden shed at the age of twelve.
Shirley Maclaine – drunk at sixteen in a New York producer's apartment.
Victoria Principal – at eighteen in the back of a blue Chevrolet.
Jerry Hall – in a hayloft at fifteen with a champion bull-rider.
Ursula Andress – at sixteen in a photographer's studio.
Curt Smith of Tears For Fears – at thirteen with an older woman from a contact magazine ad.

Allergic to Sex

An Englishman, Ian Hyman, suffered from the embarrassing complaint of sneezing every time he saw a beautiful woman. Even worse, the symptoms occured whenever he *thought* about women – which made married life extremely complicated when he suffered from a genuine cold. Mr Hyman's condition was confirmed by the Allergy and Asthma Treatment Centre in Derby, where a spokesman said: 'There is no sound basis for it except a psychological one. If he starts to sneeze just by looking at women, then the only advice is to stop.'

Some unfortunate women are allergic to sex, according to Dr I. Leonard Bernstein of Cincinnati University, who has made a special study of the subject. Symptoms can include asthma, shock, and dangerous breathing difficulties. Two women are reported to have almost died while making love. The problem lies in an allergic reaction to a protein coating on the sperm cells of their male partners.

♂ *Famous Thoughts on Sex*

'The only way to resolve a situation with a girl is to jump on her and things will work out.' **Lee Marvin.**

'A man is only as old as the woman he feels.' **Groucho Marx.**

'My passions are soccer, drinking and women – in that order.' **Rod Stewart.**

'If I were to come back in another life I'd like to be Warren Beatty's fingertips.' **Woody Allen.**

'A wife is worse than a tennis coach. At least the coach goes home in the evening.' **Ili Nastase.**

'If I'd jumped on all the dames I'm supposed to have jumped on – I'd never have had time to go fishing.' **Clark Gable.**

Embarrassing Incidents Involving Large Breasts

An Australian magazine for air-hostesses carried a medical warning urging girls not to enhance their breast size by plastic surgery. Experts believe that certain types of silicone breast implants can explode at high altitude. A sudden drop in cabin pressure has been found to make some implants rapidly expand. The risk to passengers was not revealed.

Morgana Roberts, a topless go-go dancer from Houston, Texas, was arrested for invading the pitch at a baseball game in 1985. Her lawyer apologized on her behalf and explained to the court that Morgana was leaning over the rail quietly watching the game, when her 60 in (152cm) bust caused her to overbalance and topple onto the field. During her trial for misdemeanor, the defendant spent an hour in the judge's chambers joking and signing autographs for court officials.

Waitress Siobhan Spoors was sacked from the Whistle Stop Inn at Sutton, Surrey, in 1984 because her bust was too large. When the restaurant introduced a maximum size for waitresses' uniforms Siobhan found herself out of a job because her 40 in (101cm) chest measurements required a size 16. She was awarded £1,000 after claiming sexual discrimination, in addition to receiving three proposals of marriage from total strangers and a £1,000 offer to pose nude for a magazine. One of the marriage proposals came from an Italian Count in Panama, but Siobhan announced that she intended to marry a taxi proprietor.

America's giant 3-M Company, which manufactures breast implants, faced eighty-six lawsuits totalling £30 million in 1985 from women whose breasts unexpectedly drooped. Dr Robert Kropp, a Washington plastic surgeon, received forty-three complaints from patients. He said that the worst case he encountered was that of a young woman who 'suffered spontaneous deflation' on the third day of her honeymoon. The implants were taken off the market as the company went into talks with lawyers representing women who felt badly let down.

Witnesses called to the stand during a robbery case at a Turin court all admitted difficulty in identifying one of the raiders, a girl, because she had been wearing a mask. When they agreed that her sole distinguishing feature was an extremely large bust, the judge delicately asked the defendant if she would mind unbuttoning her blouse. After some hesitation she agreed – and was immediately set free.

First Nude Calendar

A New York calender salesman made history in 1913 when he took the world's first nude calendar from his sample case. The picture, a study of a girl posing ankle deep in a lake, was a reproduction of a painting by Paul Chabas. The calendar sold so well that the Society for the Suppression of Vice demanded that a New York art gallery should cover up the original.

Original Beefcake

Britain's first male pin-up, Paul de Feu, bared all across a centre-spread in *Cosmopolitan* in April, 1972. Well, not quite all – Mr de Feu strategically arranged himself to preserve a modicum of decency. The picture was enough, however, to unleash a flood of enthusiastic poseurs. Hollywood actor Burt Reynolds followed suit within a few weeks.

♀ Famous Thoughts on Sex

'I used to be Snow White, but I drifted.' **Mae West.**

'All men are rats – and those who aren't are boring.' **Joan Collins.**

'It's been so long since I made love I can't remember who gets tied up.' **Joan Rivers.**

'Any girl can be glamorous. All you have to do is stand still and look stupid.' **Hedy Lamarr.**

'Men are like naughty little boys. They want the bar of candy they can't have. When they've got it at home, they go out and look for another piece.' **Jackie Collins.**

'Sex appeal is 50 per cent what you've got – and 50 per cent what people think you've got.' **Sophia Loren.**

DOC, BASHFUL, HAPPY
SLEEPY, SNEEZY,
GRUMPY, AND THIS IS
SEXY!

Disastrous Kisses

•Judas Iscariot.

•In 1963 downtown Rio de Janeiro was choked by a huge traffic jam caused by two teenagers locked in a passionate embrace on the front seat of their car. Traffic lights changed repeatedly, but their lips remained firmly locked together for two and a half hours. Police who fought a path through the jam quickly solved the problem. A dentist was called to disentangle the couple's dental braces.

•New York postman Arthur Heveron, apparently delighted to see his wife, kissed her so hard that his jaw locked. Doctors had to set it back into place.

•Thomas Saverland stole a kiss from Miss Caroline Newton, who responded by biting off his nose. A court acquitted her in 1837 on the grounds that: 'When a man kisses a woman against her will she is fully entitled to bite his nose, if she so pleases.' To which, the prosecuting counsel added: 'And eat it up, too!'

•A frisky plumber repaired a burst pipe at the home of Nelly Kranks in Melbourne, in 1980, and suggested that she should pay him with a kiss. Ms Kranks took a large adjustable spanner from the man's tool kit, struck him forcibly with it, and scorched him with his own blowlamp. The indignant lady then kicked the plumber down eighty-seven stairs to the ground floor, where he ran into the street begging help from pedestrians.

•A Leeds University student gave her boy-friend a kiss of such ferocity in 1983 that she ruptured his ear-drum.

•Ruth van Herpen kissed a £17,000 painting by American artist Jo Baer in an Oxford museum in 1977, 'to cheer it up because it looked so cold.' A court ordered her to pay £1,000 damages towards the cost of removing her lipstick.

•Two Egyptian students climbed the Great Pyramid of Cheops, at Giza, in 1965, with the intention of kissing at the top where there was more privacy. As they were about to embrace, the girl slipped at the summit and fell 100 ft (30 m) down the granite face. She was discharged from hospital, several weeks later, still unkissed.

Fancy Bumping into You

A forty-eight-year-old Southend woman's activities were watched by police officers who moved in and arrested her for prostitution. In court she said she could not have been soliciting in the street as she was blind in one eye and had blurred sight in the other. 'I can only see someone if they are right on top of me,' she explained.

Differences between Men and Women

- Women float better than men.
- Male stutterers outnumber female stutterers by five to one.
- Women, according to behavioural psychologists, tend to strike matches away from themselves. Men strike matches towards them.
- A man's brain weighs on average 4 oz (113g) more than a woman's. This is no indication of greater intelligence.
- Women are four times more likely than men to reach the age of 100.
- Twice as many women as men diet.
- The Medical Research Council discovered that women, on average, sleep twenty-five minutes a night longer than men.
- Women tend to have slightly better hearing than men.
- Most men tie an apron at the front; women usually tie them at the back.
- Women take fewer risks crossing the road and use zebra crossings more than men, according to studies carried out at the Road Research Laboratory.

Greatest Mass Streak

The thunder of 1,200 naked Americans on the hoof shook the dusty ground of Boulder, Colorado, in 1974, when the starting gun was fired for what is claimed to be the world's largest mass streak. It narrowly beat the record of 1,000 students from Athens, Georgia, who streaked together earlier the same year.

Historical Figures who Contracted VD

Ivan the Terrible
Keats
Hitler
Abraham
Boswell
Oscar Wilde
Gauguin
Albrecht Durer
Pope Julius II
John of Gaunt (though the disease had no bearing on his name!)

Selling Yourself

Marcel Winters, a thirty-four-year-old clerk from Sydney, Australia, spent £2,500 on a glossy brochure promoting his finer points in an attempt to find a partner. He resorted to the rather drastic move after six failed love affairs. The brochure featured a picture of Marcel boarding a bus, with the caption: 'If you'd like to be cruising in an expensive car, forget it. If you go out with Marcel, this is how you will travel.'

The Marcel promotion was aimed specifically at girls with big busts and bottoms, 'the bigger the better', and thighs 'like a tennis player'. They were expected, however, to acquire Marcel's frugal tastes. There would be no diamonds or champagne, and engagement rings were 'high-priced rubbish for wealthy materialists'. The brochure elicited fifty replies but, perhaps unsurprisingly, none met his exacting standards.

A thirty-six-year-old anonymous Los Angeles man paid $1,200 to have a movie short thrown onto the screen of his local cinema. It was called 'What Do You Think Of My Face?' and included his telephone number. The advertisement resulted in 1,000 telephone calls – none, alas, from a suitable partner.

Once a year in the tiny Indian village of Saurath the world's biggest marriage market opens for business – selling prospective husbands. They line up for inspection in their thousands to be prodded and cross-questioned by 100,000 critical women. Prices at the week-long sale begin at £200, but more expensive models command up to £12,000. Haggling can take the best part of a day, but more than 2,000 couples depart together each year.

Granny Betty Bolen combed Toledo, Ohio, for two years looking for her Mr Right. The mother of three, who also has five grandchildren, had no success until she placed an advertisement in her local paper.

It read: 'Ugly woman, forty-seven, drinks and smokes with no redeeming qualities. Wants to meet nice-looking rich man. Can be plain-looking, average income, maybe ugly and unemployed, or any of the above.'

Betty was swamped with replies and finally chose a burly giant called Bill. 'I wasn't looking for somebody perfect,' she smiled. 'But maybe I found him.'

Tongue-tied New Yorkers pour out their hearts to the object of their affection through the gushing pen of Deborah Lehmann. As the head of Love Letters Anonymous she writes extremely passionate letters for those who find it hard to express their feelings. Deborah, a born romantic, keeps her own feet firmly on the ground. The charge for a throbbing epistle is $15.

LOVERS LANE
POPE MOBILE

• *Pope John* XII
An unruly tenth-century teenager who was made Pontiff at the age of eighteen. He had a voracious sexual appetite and was accused of turning the Papal palace into a brothel and raping women pilgrims. He was finally caught making love to a married woman and beaten to death by her husband.

• *Pope Sergius* III
One result of his many conquests was an illegitimate son whom he ordered to be installed as his successor.

• *Pope Leo* VIII
A Holy Father who died in unusual circumstances – he was seized by a mysterious paralysis and expired while having intercourse with a married woman.

• *Pope Alexander* VI
A pontiff whose favourite recreation appears to have been organizing orgies for the Papal Assembly. On one lavish occasion naked girls danced and there were prizes for guests who managed to have intercourse with the greatest number of prostitutes.

• *Pope Benedict* IX
He began his Papal career at the tender age of ten and soon after embarked on a lifetime of debauchery which 'shocked the sensibilities even of a dull and barbarous age.'

• *Pope Balthasar Cossa*
Incest and adultery were among his favourite pastimes. The only official toll of his activities – thought to be a modest estimate – was 200 women, including 'nuns, widows and matrons.'

The Most Lavish Orgy of the Eighties

Police investigating the books of New York's most expensive madam in 1984, came across an account of a party-loving Saudi prince who spent £100,000 on a single night out. He hired thirty £1,000-a-night girls from Sydney Bibble Barrows high-class brothel, and took them along with nine friends and relatives to ten £1,500-a-day suites at the Waldorf Towers Hotel. First they feasted on a £30,000 meal at Rejine's on Park Avenue; then they prepared for bed with their chosen partners after firing corks from dozens of Dom Perignon champagne bottles at each other.

Romantic Encounters Which Ended in the Arms of the Law

In 1984 a beautiful girl was seduced by the smooth-talk of a young man in a Swansea pub. He plied her with drinks and at closing time took her home to a luxurious housing estate. They slept together, but next morning she woke alone to find herself, rather like Snow White, surrounded by curious staff in a show house. 'We took some drinks back and made love,' the embarrassed girl explained. 'When I woke he was getting dressed. He said he was on the early shift and told me to go back to sleep.'

When postmaster Michele Di Meglio fell in love with postmistress Annamaria Tolmat, messages winged the 500 miles (804 km) between their two offices via the Italian State Telex Service; teleprinters rattled incessantly with tender endearments. Seven years after the start of their affair and 18,000 words of affection later the couple were caught by Post Office investigators who discovered that none of the messages had been paid for.

At their trial for the 'illegal use of State telecommunications' the judge heard how their passionate telexes had choked official communication lines throughout the whole of

SHOW HOUSE
OF
ILL-REPUTE

the Fuili region, even when emergency services were trying to deal with an earthquake. Obviously a serious business, but this, after all, was Italy – a country renowned for its passion. The judge worked out the standard rate of telex charges and halved it because they were in love. They were fined £500 each, but Di Meglio had to face the real penalty – his wife was waiting for him at home with a broom handle.

A lift which ran up the outside of a fifty-storey Atlanta skyscraper was built to give a panoramic view of the city. Two passengers, Tammie Diedrich, nineteen, and twenty-seven-year-old Charles Skelton were so engrossed in each other that they completely forgot that the walls were made of glass. As the lift rose they stripped off and began to make love, bringing traffic to a standstill. By the time the lift had made its slow descent police were waiting to charge them with public indecency.

Police called by neighbours to a flat in Oslo in 1982 found Olaf Fredericksen tickling his wife Astrid. Mrs Fredericksen confessed that she adored it, but it made her scream uncontrollably.

The Orient Express was delayed for forty minutes at Innsbruck in September 1984 while engineers and railway officials combed the train to discover how the emergency brakes had suddenly been applied. All was revealed when they opened the door of a private sleeping compartment and came across a couple making love. The woman's foot, in a moment of ecstasy, had pressed the emergency-stop lever, bringing the train to an unscheduled halt.

A British Airways stewardess had an unusual sexual arrangement with her husband before she left on short-hop trips. To satisfy his penchant for bondage she would leave him tied up and naked in the bedroom wardrobe, returning to release him after the six-hour return journey to Paris. All went well until the plane was delayed in August 1984, when she was

ORIENT EXPRESS?
THAT'LL DO NICELY!
PLATFORM 12
ORIENT EXPRESS

told that she could not return to Heathrow until the following morning. The distraught stewardess, according to Gatwick Airport's staff magazine, *Skyport,* had to telephone the Metropolitan Police to break into their home and release him.

Highway patrols in Cooperville, Texas, set up armed roadblocks when a man was spotted driving a car with a woman blindfolded in the passenger seat. He was pulled up at gunpoint and the woman was led to safety by police who ignored the driver's protests that he was taking his wife to a surprise birthday treat at an expensive resturant.

Business as Usual

When book-keeper Herbert Muller's firm went out of business, leaving him redundant, he could not bear to break the news to his wife. Each day he left for work as usual and at the end of the week he handed her his pay as though nothing had changed.

Herbert, desperate for a job, had embarked on a second career. It began when he placed an ad in a magazine: 'Gentleman will make housecalls to satisfy even hard-to-please ladies.' The word spread round a circle of wealthy women in his home town of Dusseldorf and humble Herbert became an overnight sensation.

Mrs Muller continued to receive her weekly housekeeping, but sensed that life was somehow not quite the same. 'He was always whacked.' she told a divorce court judge. 'It was always "Not tonight Elsa – I'm too tired."' The truth emerged when she visited the office to complain to Herbert's boss that he was being worked too hard, and found the building boarded up.

Back home she went through his pockets and to her amazement found a detailed list of his clients and their unusual sexual requirements. The couple were last heard of trying for a reconciliation.

Holiday Mishaps

British building worker Caldwell Macguire, jailed for making love to a topless sunbather on a crowded Greek beach, protested his innocence. Crowds lined the harbour breakwater at Nafplion, jostling for a view, until the couple were arrested and charged with 'provoking a scandal by indecent public acts'. Mr Caldwell explained his behaviour with Agnes Wright by claiming: 'I was just giving her the kiss of life'.

Peter Levy, a Rotterdam engineer, took a caravan holiday in Spain with his wife in 1984. As she drove gingerly through Barcelona's rush-hour traffic, Peter stripped off in the caravan for a wash. Mrs Levy, spying a gap in the traffic, suddenly put her foot down, and her husband was catapulted completely naked into the street. Peak-hour crowds gathered chanting 'Ole!' as Mr Levy lunged wildly at a vegetable stall to cover his front and rear with cabbage leaves. His ordeal ended when police bundled him into a car and caught up with his wife.

Jeff Corwin, thirty-one, and his girl-friend Laurie Zyburo, twenty-one, lay locked together on Cedar Beach, Long Island, oblivious to the cares of the world. As they kissed and cuddled in the sand, a 4-ton dumper truck rumbled into view and ran over them. Incredibly the couple were pushed into the soft sand, and sat up completely uninjured, except for tyre marks across their faces.

Happily-married James Hardy, fifty-six, walked into the bedroom of his Ohio hotel and encountered a half-naked, extremely attractive blonde. Mr Hardy averted his head so sharply that he slipped a disc and had to undergo surgery to correct his posture. He successfully sued the hotel for handing him the wrong key and was awarded $25,000.

As darkness fell over Majorca, factory worker Jose Aguilea prepared himself for a night on the town in search of female company. He stepped into the shower in his hotel room and

encountered it sooner than expected. Twenty-eight-stone (178 kg) Jose crashed through the floor into the room below and staggered unhurt from the rubble to face two horrified girls. 'I'm going to put myself on a diet,' he explained.

Femmes Fatal

Professor Jean-Paul Broustet, of Bordeaux University, warned middle-aged French husbands in 1984 that having an affair can seriously damage your health. Four out of five cases of heart attacks during love-making happened to couples who were not married to each other, he said. Professor Broustet explained that when a middle-aged man makes love to his wife it is equivalent to climbing three floors. 'But with a girl-friend it is like racing up the stairs of a skyscraper, or sprinting three miles,' he warned.

Revealing Footwear

A 1986 survey by leading psychologists in West Germany concluded that you can tell a great deal about a man from the shoes he wears.

- Men who wear pointed-toed shoes tend to be good lovers with plenty of sexual experience.
- Men who wear sensible lace-up shoes tend to think too much about work to be considerate lovers, and are reluctant to share household chores.
- Men who relax in jogging shoes are less carefree than their appearance suggests. Their sexual attraction is often marred by a preoccupation with health problems.

• *Potatoes*
The humble spud was greatly acclaimed by Dr Cyril Daly in 1984, when he described it in the *Irish Medical Times* as 'a godsend to Irish sexuality.' He gave potatoes credit for the eighteenth-century population boom and expressed surprise that anyone could regard them as 'a simple culinary irrelevance.' In Dr Daly's opinion 'the potato is a passionate and violent tuber carrying within its sightless eyes memories of violence, death and sexuality.' Begorra.

• *Stags' Tails*
The Scots can hardly believe that they once threw them away. Game dealers now sell them to Hong Kong for £2 each in what has become a booming export market. Demand is so great that poachers have moved in. When a man was fined £100 for stealing £600 worth of stags' tails from Grantown-on-Spey in 1984, his solicitor dryly remarked: 'If stags' tails had aphrodisiac properties I would have thought that Scotsmen would have discovered that years ago and kept the secret to themselves.'

• *Water*
Spanish medical papers reported an undignified rush to bottle the waters from a natural spring in Alanje in 1901. The man who discovered its properties, Dr Martinez Reguiera, claimed that taking the waters would 'allay the pangs of one-sided affection.'

Water containing traces of radioactivity from a spa at Luchon, in the Pyrenees, was claimed to have similar properties in 1960. Dr Grandpierre of the French Air Force Medical Corps lifted the skirts of obliging female patients and ran a Geiger counter up their legs, to discover which parts of the body radioactivity spread to, or so the good doctor claimed.

APHRODISIAC!
APHRODISIAC!

•*Chocolate*
Powdered chocolate is one of the favourite bases of fake aphrodisiacs – an old Algerian made a fortune overnight in 1957 selling packets of the stuff to the American Sixth Fleet off Cannes, before he was arrested. Ironically, chocolates themselves have undeniably romantic connotations. The reason, say Dr Heine Baume and Dr Jeanette Dogny of Hamburg, is phenethylamine – an essential ingredient in human sexual chemistry, produced naturally by our bodies and also found in chocolate. A mug of cocoa may be the perfect nightcap, after all.

•*Pickled Worms*
Mezcal, a golden Mexican liqueur guaranteed to contain a pickled worm in the bottom of each bottle, is sold all over the world. When supplies reached Trowbridge, Wiltshire, in 1983, local shopkeeper Mac Matharu found it hard to believe the demand. Locals claimed that the flavour of the white 2-in (5cm) long worm made a dramatic improvement to their love-lives. 'People kept coming back for more bottles with big smiles on their faces,' Mr Matharu reported. 'There is nothing unhygienic about it. The worm probably died of alcoholism and is well-pickled.'

•*Newts*
A popular aphrodisiac in Japan. The technique is to burn them, divide the ashes into two, pocketing one portion and sprinkling the remainder over the hair of the lady of your choice.

•*Spanish Fly*
Cantharides, or Spanish fly as it is better known, is an extract of small Iberian beetles, hailed for its potent properties. Scientific doubt is cast on its claims, but Cabrol the sixteenth-century French physician came across an intriguing case from Provence. A woman who had given her husband cantharides for a fever was surprised when he made a miraculous recovery

and made love to her eighty-seven times in two nights. Cabrol added that gangrene then set into his penis and he expired.

• *Gallstones*
A cold storage plant in Bulawayo helps to boost Zimbabwe's balance of payments by exporting gallstones from cattle to the Far East where they are highly prized as aphrodisiacs.

A Ticklish Situation

Women living on the Uganda-Sudan border sexually arouse their men by tickling them under the armpits.

Endangered Species

One of the puzzling problems of the veterinary world is a frustrating condition found in some bulls called 'corkscrew penis'. The unfortunate animal suffers the indignity of its penis suddenly twisting itself into a corkscrew shape seconds before copulation, thus preventing penetration.

Staff at Bristol Zoo were anxious to swell the numbers of their penguin colony, but despite every inducement nothing could persuade the birds to mate. Zoo keepers finally called in a penguin expert who tactfully pointed out that all the birds were female.

Edinburgh Zoo came to the rescue with some male birds. 'It's not easy to tell the sex of a penguin – unless you are another penguin,' said a spokesman.

Odd Indecency Cases

An Ohio judge dismissed an indecency case brought against stripper Melinda Safian in 1985 because her act failed to sexually arouse the arresting vice-squad detective. When Detective Ron Ziolkowski of Toledo described her stage act in intimate detail the judge told him: 'The arousal factor is essential in proving that her performance appeals to your prurient interest.' Unless the officer experienced 'lustful thought or desire' there was no obscenity involved.

Miss Safian left the court more worried than delighted. 'I'm not sure whether I gained or not,' she said. Meanwhile, back at vice-squad headquarters, a furious Captain Derwish Mohamed declared: 'Next time I'll find an officer who gets more excited by those sort of shows.'

A judge and jury in San Fernando, Chile, asked the accused, exotic dancer Mavisa Lonez, for a courtroom demonstration of her act, which police claimed was indecent. Mavisa obligingly put on a record and launched into her suggestive routine.

At the conclusion of an outstanding performance the jury jumped to its feet and burst into spontaneous cheering and applause. The judge warmly thanked Mavisa for her efforts and the court settle down to deliver its verdict: fined £25 for indecency.

Films and magazines ruled obscene by an Idaho judge were supposed to be the main exhibit in a case against two bookstores – until the evidence mysteriously went missing 'while under the care of the United States Supreme Court.' No one would admit responsibility, but someone had enough sexy reading and viewing to last for years.

THE COURT WILL... ER ...RISE!

Tales of Passionate Pensioners

Evaristo Bertone, an eighty-five-year-old Sicilian, flew into a blind rage when he discovered a passionate love-letter addressed to his wife Adriana. The thought that she was unfaithful after years of marriage was more than he could stand. Evaristo picked up a knife and stabbed his partner in the shoulder. When he showed her the offending letter she pointed out that he had written it himself half a century earlier. Adriana said: 'His eyesight is so poor these days that I forgave him.'

Fists flew at a north London Darby and Joan tea dance when Benjamin Shulman, sixty-three, saw someone make a pass at his blonde dancing partner, Mrs Olga Raab. As the band played 'I Only Have Eyes For You,' he grabbed Leonard Bloomberg, fifty-two, and gave him a black eye.

Mr Bloomberg, who denied placing a hand on Mrs Raab's thigh, said: 'It was ridiculous. She came in and I said hello. Mr Shulman punched me viciously in the right eye.' Mr Shulman was fined £50 for assault.

A seventy-seven-year-old Cardiff pensioner, David Philips, was fined £5 in 1975 for snatching kisses from forty-two patrolling female traffic wardens.

A Late Developer

Mae West ('Come up and see me – I've nothing on but the radio') endured as a Hollywood star to a ripe old age, but amazingly only began making pictures and became acknowledged as a sex goddess at the age of forty.

•If the eldest child in the family is a girl, studies show that she is likely to grow up with the most sex appeal.

•It is possible to become hooked on sex, like drugs or alcohol. Self-help groups called Sexaholics Anonymous exist in America.

•Looks are important in sex appeal, but men and women usually end up choosing a mate with the same IQ as themselves.

•Despite all the songs, studies show that the moon – even in June – does not make the slightest difference to romance or sex drive.

•The National Marriage Guidance Council says that backseat sex sessions in cars can lead to unhappy relationships. Anxiety about being caught can linger into later life.

•Sex was placed fourteenth on a list of favourite occupations by Americans – lower than house repairs and gardening.

•Sex once a week is the average for most British couples, according to 2,000 women who answered a questionnaire.

•Women with beautiful figures have less self-confidence than plain-Janes. Arizona University researchers found that having a perfect body led only to greater anxiety about it.

•Too much sex can be bad for your love life, according to Rome doctor William Pasini. He suggests that six months' total abstinence can work wonders for a jaded marriage.

•When 300 women were asked what colour hair they preferred in men, 65 per cent chose dark hair, and only 18 per cent preferred blonds.

•Men need women more than women need men. A survey of 30,000 people revealed that men are much more bored, disorganized and lonely without a mate than women.

•Tranquillizers are thought to be the cause of several sexual problems, including lack of sex drive.

•A survey by the US Government Health Service revealed that only 6 per cent of middle-aged men up to the age of sixty-nine had lost interest in sex, compared with 33 per cent of women.

IT DOESN'T MAKE YOU RANDY... IT JUST CURES HEADACHES!
LOVE POTION

•Vitamin A can give your sex life a boost according to researchers at the Fresh Fruit and Vegetable Bureau. It converts cholesterol into active sex hormones, they say.
•In an eight-hour test, sex researchers put a full-length mirror in a Munich department store. A third of the 1,620 women who passed it glanced at themselves. All of the 600 men walking by paused to admire themselves.
•Spring isn't when men's fancy lightly turns to thoughts of love – their highest hormone production point is in winter.
•Falling in love can bring on headaches, rashes and colds, according to the GP's newspaper, *Doctor*.
•Love at first sight is a scientific fact – boffins blame it on neurons, or brain cells, which match up what we see with pleasant past experiences.
•According to *Which?* magazine dating agencies are a waste of time for one in three lonely hearts.
•Finally – how much do we worry about all those sex surveys? Austrian sexologist Ernest Borneman claims they are useless because most lovers tend to exaggerate their performance, or generally lie to questions.

Well I Never!

The first International Conference on Love and Attraction thought it important to begin with an offical definition of love. This is how the experts see it: 'The cognitive-affective state characterized by intrusive and obsessive fantasizing concerning reciprocity and amorant feeling by the object of the amorance.' More concise, less qualified people have reduced it to four letters.

Unusual Valentine Messages

- A bunch of dead flowers to tell someone I Don't Love You Anymore are available from American Michael Hirsch. He will deliver 'a dozen carelessly picked' wilted roses bound with a black silk ribbon.
- Selfridges of London sell embossing stamps for Valentine's Day which punch I Love You into slices of breakfast toast.
- Air advertising companies offer special romantic Valentine messages which can be towed behind a plane for £300.
- To tell the world you love someone in neon lights across Piccadilly Circus can be arranged for anyone with £10,000 to spare.
- For an average cost of £30 each you can declare your love while free-falling from 12,000 ft (3658 m). The use of a two-way radio – essential under the circumstances – is extra.
- The hire of advertising billboards to display personal Valentine messages is becoming increasingly popular. A prime site in Trafalgar Square costs £1,500.

Record Number of Lovers

There have been many contenders for the title, but perhaps few who could compete with a New York hooker who, according to the *Lancet* in 1983, had 15,000 lovers. She worked only three months in every twelve, but had an estimated twenty-four clients a day when on duty. Her sex marathon came to light in a survey backed by New York City health department. Eventually, as a result of excessive sex, her body resistance to disease broke down.

Sexy Facts about Feet

Catherine the Great of Russia got great sexual pleasure from having her feet tickled.
•A Japanese study of eighteenth-century erotic art revealed that women expressed satisfaction after sex by curling their toes.
•Dr Glen Wilson, a psychologist at the University of London, believes that men who leave their socks on during sex show signs of insecurity.
•The relationship between colour choice and personality, pioneered by Dr Max Luscher, suggests that red socks indicate a strong sexual drive.
•Screen star Sophia Loren says that she derives great sensual pleasure from rolling her bare feet over a wooden rolling-pin while watching television.
•For centuries women had their feet bound in China because small feet were considered a great sexual attribute.

Minority Sexual Attractions

•*Military Uniforms*
There was something about a soldier that blonde Patricia Smith found hard to resist – she married six of them in as many years. But only three of her marriages to men in khaki were legal. In fact the twenty-nine-year-old bigamist was so desperate to marry her last husband, a Royal Engineer, that she approached two strangers in a pub and asked them to be witnesses.

When magistrates at Harrogate, Yorkshire, gave Patricia six months marching orders, she pleaded: 'I was only looking for a stable home.'

• *Bearded Ladies*
When it comes to sexual attraction there are men who swear that bearded ladies win by a whisker. Professional bearded ladies, once familiar in travelling freak shows, are a rarity in Britain. A few still appear with European circuses, but Germany, strangely, remains the world stronghold of the bearded lady. One of the most famous, Barbara Urileria, had to fight off prospective lovers wherever she appeared.

In the seventeenth century a Belgian bearded lady, Helene Antonia, sported a set of whiskers down to her navel. One of her contemporaries observed: 'The number of men who love her is legion.'

• *High-heeled Shoes*
Ronald George of Islington, London, got an overwhelming kick from high-heeled shoes. To obtain fresh supplies he stopped women in the street and offered to clean their shoes, claiming that they were dirty. As soon as they slipped them off he snatched up the footwear and ran away. George even flagged down women motorists to tell them they had an oil leak which he then offered to repair using the heel of their shoe. He was eventually brought to heel and charged with stealing shoes worth £689.

• *Three-legged Men*
Francesco Lentini was born with three legs and grew up to make a successful living exhibiting himself in short trousers. His future looked assured until a wealthy Central European lady set eyes on him. Her passions were so aroused that she arranged to have Francesco kidnapped to keep him for herself. After a long period of imprisonment he managed to flee the love-nest she had built and resume his career on the exhibition circuit.

FAIR
PERFUME
AFTER SHAVE

WE ARE NOT AMUSED!
SQUAT NOW

•*Sailors*
Every week for eight years after leaving school, a Marseilles shop-girl, Jocelyne Versois-Marchienne, sat down and wrote letters to 140 lovesick sailors. One day the correspondence abruptly stopped – Jocelyne announced that she had fallen in love with a soldier.

•*Spectacles*
A London postman could not resist making passes at girls who wore glasses. Unfortunately they all looked down their nose at him when they discovered it was their spectacles he was after. Over a two-year period he snatched thirty-eight pairs of glasses from girls he found attractive. When he appeared in court charged with robbery, a psychiatrist estimated that it would take at least five years' treatment to see him right.

Books with Unfortunate Titles

The Handbook For Fitters Of Camp Supports (Jackson, 1938)
The Gentle Art Of Cooking Wives (Dodge, 1900)
Gay Bulgaria (Hale, 1964)
Fun On The Billiard Table (Pearson, 1899)
How Nell Scored (Nelson, 1929)
Wife Battering: A Systems Theory Approach (Guilford Press, 1983)
Every Inch A Sailor (Nelson, 1897)
Ten Good Tricks With Empty Bass Bottles (Bass Ltd, 1929)
Recollections Of Squatting In Victoria (Melbourne University Press, 1965)
Dildo Kay (Hoghton Mifflin, 1940)

From Russell Ash and Brian Lake's collection of bizarre books.

The first four minutes at the breakfast table and the first four minutes after arriving home from work are the flashpoint for three-quarters of all serious rows between married couples, according to an American psychologist. People should think carefully before they speak, he says, because these are the times when we are at a low ebb, edgy, drained and touchy.

In a study of domestic murders it was found that women tend to kill their husbands in the kitchen, while men prefer the bedroom.

There was a sizzling row when Paul Gosburger accused his wife of undercooking his sausages. A divorce court judge at Great Falls, Montana, heard that Mrs Gosburger struck back. She stormed out of the kitchen and triumphantly sat on her husband's matchstick model of the Statue of Liberty which had taken him five years to complete. After that, of course, the marriage was in splinters.

New Yorker Zaza Kimmont walked into the bathroom and noticed a strange toothbrush next to her husband's. She snatched it up and examined it minutely – there was no mistaking traces of lipstick on the bristles. Zaza flew into a rage and wrecked the house, throwing everything breakable at the walls, sweeping ornaments from shelves and overturning furniture. She stormed out to her mother's leaving £5,000 worth of damage in her wake. There she learned that her mother-in-law had been to stay while she was away, and had left her toothbrush behind.

Divorce lawyers drew up a unique two-year legal contract to save a marriage by making the husband do less housework. The couple – named only as Karl and Charlotte – appeared to have the perfect marriage. Karl, a forty-one-year-old clerk, cooked the meals, took his wife breakfast on a tray, washed the dishes, put the children to bed, ironed, darned socks and

I'M IN THE BEDROOM, HONEY!
I'M IN THE KITCHEN, DARLING!

sewed. When he started knitting it was more than Charlotte could stand. She went off sex and consulted her lawyers. 'I can't stand a man who never does anything wrong,' she told them. 'If only he'd go to the pub once in a while.' The couple from Bielefeld, West Germany, have agreed to share housework equally until 1988.

Half My Worldly Goods

Eugene Schneider objected when a divorce court judge in Carteret, New Jersey, ordered him to divide his property equally with his wife. When the judge insisted that the order of the court would have to be carried out, Schneider took his chain saw and cut their £40,000 wooden bungalow down the middle.

Man-handle

In 1986, after a three-year court battle, Miss Ellen Cooperman, a member of the National Organization for Women, won the legal right to call herself Ms Ellen Cooperson.

Persistent Lovers

Charles Radclyffe, the Fifth Earl of Derwentwater, was rejected no less than fifteen times by the Countess of Newburgh, who finally ordered her staff to lock all the doors and ban him from the house for ever. The indefatigible earl climbed down her chimney and proposed to her covered in soot. She accepted.

A twenty-seven-year-old Birmingham office worker could not take his eyes off the new typist who had joined the firm.

He asked the eighteen-year-old for a date, but she turned him down. He found it hard to take no for an answer and pestered her so much that she handed in her resignation.

Even then he bombarded her with more than 100 love letters, some signed in his own blood. For the next four years he doggedly followed her, despite the fact that she was engaged to someone else and was planning her wedding. After three court appearances and a tough warning from magistrates his ardour cooled. But after all that time the flame had not completely extinguished. 'It was hopeless from the start – but I still love her,' he admitted.

A tongue-tied St Albans garage hand worked out an elaborate plan to attract the attention of an attractive girl he had seen driving around town. He would sabotage the engine of her car while she was in a local wine bar. Then, as she struggled to get it started, he would just happen to pass by carrying his tool box and come to the rescue.

Unfortunately she walked out of the wine bar while he was still trying to immobilize her engine – and she was not alone. Her policeman boy-friend took a keen interest in his activities. After being fined £40 the Romeo mechanic said: 'I could not think of any other way to get a date.'

Frederick Sales was a sucker for the sweet smile of a door-to-door cosmetics sales girl who rang the bell of his New York apartment. To attract her interest he placed order after order each Tuesday so that she would return. Sales became so smitten that he stole from his employers to pay for the £5,000 worth of cosmetics he bought over three years. When he ran out of money police found the goods still wrapped in his bedroom.

After being fined £100 Sales explained: 'She was so lovely, I didn't have the heart to turn her down.'

The Council that Thinks of Everything

Civic leaders in Grand Rapids, Michigan, extended their equality rules to strip joints. At ratepayers' expense all strip-tease clubs have had ramps built in the wings to enable handicapped strippers to take their wheelchairs on stage.

The Sexiest Girls' Names

Researchers conducting a poll among college students in New York asked them to think carefully of the sexiest girls' names. These were the results:

1 Christine
2 Candice
3 Cheryl
4 Melanie
5 Dawn
6 Heather
7 Jennifer
8 Marilyn
9 Michelle
10 Susan

The Most Sexually Unattractive Girls' Names

The same New York students were then asked to give the biggest turn-offs. They were:

1 Ethel
2 Elvira
3 Eurolinda
4 Edna
5 Alma
6 Florence
7 Mildred
8 Myrtle
9 Silvana

Jon Jennings, who lives in the Philippines, was sorry he opened his big mouth. In the course of twelve months he promised to marry six different women. When he failed to do so, the furious girls beat him up.

When, a year later, he had still not exchanged vows with any of them, the girls beat him so badly that he had to be admitted to hospital. The last news from the Philippines was that he still had not made his mind up.

Conman Rudi Hartmann paraded around with a chestful of fake medals, telling women he was a widowered NATO general to persuade them to part with their money. Over 300 women across Germany were swindled out of their savings by the phoney general.

When it came to love however, Rudi, forty-seven, was denounced by his victims as a total flop. He boasted that he was a superman between the sheets, but whenever he reached the bedroom door he always made an excuse and left. 'Not tonight,' he would say, 'I've got a splitting headache.' Another favourite excuse was that he was too drunk. Even when a thirty-three-year-old blonde named Ella climbed naked into his bed he was a wash-out. She told police: 'He said he had taken special pills while on a secret mission and could not make whoopee until they wore off.'

Blessed with a memory like a sieve, two-timing romeo Janos Istvan really should have known better. On Mondays, Wednesdays and Fridays he slept at home with his wife. Tuesdays and Thursdays were nights of passion with girl-friend number one; while weekends were spent curled up with girl-friend number two.

But his memory was so bad that he kept getting their names mixed up. To avoid an embarrassing slip-up he persuaded them all to change their name to Rosy; and when each Rosy bore him a son he called each baby Stefan. He managed to muddle through for four years, roaring from one woman to

....AND WHAT DID YOU GET THIS ONE FOR?

MY LIFE **FLASHED** IN FRONT OF ME!

another on his motor-cycle. But his lifestyle was doomed from the outset. When his wife Rosy was cleaning his motor-cycle one day she found an address book with the birthdays and telephone numbers of the other Rosy's and Stefans. Within hours the three women had met – a meeting which was to end in the German divorce court. Janos' wife divorced him, while Rosy II and III sued for maintenance. Janos, thirty-nine, said after the hearing: 'I should have remembered to take that list out of my saddle-bag.'

Little could be said to Dieter Mayer's credit, except for the fact that he had sharp reflexes. When his lover's husband came home unexpectedly he grabbed his clothes and made a lightning dive under the bed. He remained there, shivering, waiting to roll out when the coast was clear and make his escape into the Innsbruck night.

It was a long wait. The husband, almost twice the size of diminutive Dieter, stayed in the bedroom watching TV, reading and smoking . . . for a mind-boggling thirty-nine hours.

At last he went out. Dieter, shaking from exposure and barely able to move, dragged himself from his hiding place – just as the husband walked back into the room looking for his keys. He picked up the unfortunate romeo and hit him so hard that his front teeth were knocked out and his vision temporarily impaired.

In extreme danger they say that a man's life often flashes before him. Spanish waiter Armando Verez confirms that this is true. He arrived at the church for his wedding to find his lovely bride-to-be waiting at the altar . . . flanked by the eight fiancees he had jilted in the preceding four years.

The irate girls brandished cast-iron saucepans and were clearly thirsting for justice. Armando fled and hammered for sanctuary on the door of a nearby police station. The wedding, of course, was cancelled.

Romance Makes a Come-back

There are signs that promiscuous sex is giving way to old-fashioned romance. New York research psychologist Srully Blotnick believes that the reason is a growing fear of disease. He has surveyed 12,000 single men and women since 1966 and finds that attitudes have changed. Twenty years ago 75.3 per cent of men and 39.1 per cent of women 'liked the idea of casual sex.' Now only 55 per cent of men and 23 per cent of women find it appealing.

Ideal Women Around the World

L'Oreal, the French cosmetics company, conducted a two-year study to discover the ideal woman, and found that ideas differ widely around the world.

• *England*
Researchers found that Englishmen spend more time with male chums than possibly any other nation. Accordingly, women are expected to keep a low profile and preferably to be ladylike rather than sexy in public.

• *Germany*
Men in Germany like women to be masculine, the kind who can almost make them crawl. According to a L'Oreal spokeswoman: 'German women must be aggressive, have long hair, be healthy and well-shaped.' Which almost perfectly describes the German World Cup squad.

• *United States*
American men tend not to like assertive women, or women more intelligent than themselves. If they are, they prefer them not to admit to it. Their ideal woman has 'an ample bust and long, glamorous hair.'

•*Italy*
Researchers found that women are expected to dress like movie stars with as much make-up as possible, perfumes, chains, bracelets and dresses which exaggerate the female form.

'Sophia Loren is the best example of the type of woman attractive to Italian men. She is almost a goddess, with big breasts and big, child-bearing hips.'

•*Norway*
Norwegian men, by contrast, have a functional outlook. Women are ideally blonde, tall, sporty, fond of drinking and never wear make-up.

•*Japan*
Japanese men, strangely to Western tastes, do not care about a woman's figure. 'The face and neck are very sexy,' says L'Oreal. 'A woman must put her hair up to show her neck. If she leaves it down she is considered dirty – and cleanliness is very important.'

•*Spain*
Spanish women should preferably consider themselves superior to men, and be capable of seducing with their eyes. Hair should be long, and clothes tightly fitted to reveal the shape of the body.

•*France*
The French are attracted to the capable career woman, elegant with slim legs, and preferably a good mother. With a wife who goes out to work, manages to look chic *and* looks after the children, French men appear to want the best of everything with the minumum personal effort.

A Beautiful Move

Women in Ugley, Bedfordshire, felt embarrassed about the name of their local organization, the Ugley Women's Institute. It has since been changed to the Women's Institute (Ugley Division).

Hot Chocolate

In Santa Cruz, California, a woman acquired a fixation for her next door neighbour. He was happily married, but she still tried to seduce him by various mean, all of which failed. Then, obsessed with getting him into bed, she played her final card – a ploy which hinged heavily on his fondness for chocolate.

As the man returned from the office and was putting his key in the front door, the woman leapt from behind a bush, completely naked and covered from head to foot in melted chocolate. The man recoiled in horror as she threw her arms around him and smothered him in a gooey embrace. His wife happened to look out of the window and called the police, who took the neighbour away for a short rest in a local psychiatric hospital.

Convincing Conmen

In 1984 a housewife in Teaneck, New Jersey, had a phone call from a man who informed her that he was her husband's sex therapist and was anxious to enlist her help. The newly-wed wife was happy to oblige, even when the caller instructed her to walk out of the house and have sex with the first stranger she met.

The twenty-five-year-old woman dutifully ran into the garden and asked her next-door neighbour to come to bed. An hour later, when her husband returned from work, she could not wait to tell him how she had helped. The dumbfounded man recovered from shock sufficiently to tell her: 'I haven't got a sex therapist.' He then raced next door threatening to kill his new neighbour.

Police were called in to tap the phone. Six days later, after a second call, they arrested the vice-president of the company which owns the Harlem Globetrotters basketball team and charged him with sexual harassment.

A plausible pest in the Midlands went from door-to-door posing as a council medical officer and smooth-talked housewives into stripping off for an examination. He was so convincing that when one of their husbands unexpectedly arrived home, he cooly talked him into stripping off too.

The youngest sex-hoaxer on record was a sixth-form schoolboy who stole the school doctor's stethoscope, borrowed his father's car and roared off in the direction of the local girls' grammar school, dressed in a white coat.

A psychologist who dealt with the case said: 'He talked the matron into providing him with facilities to examine young girls. He spent a happy morning among them and would doubtless have escaped if one of his "patients" had not recognized him. He was referred to me – but it was the hysterical headmistress who needed most attention.'

Gays on the March

The tramp of 10,000 heavily-armed gays on the march was a familiar sight in ancient times. The Sacred Band of Thebes was composed of gay troops who fought alongside their lovers to prove their courage. They were formidable fighters, led by Greek general Xenophon (motto: 'People who do not choose handsome men for the command of their troops are mad.')

Cases of Adventurous Sex

In 1981 crowds of shoppers in a Montevideo market stared in astonishment as a middle-aged couple lay down behind the stalls and had intercourse in the gutter. A court later decided to dismiss a charge of indecency when they explained that their doctor had told them to introduce as much variety as possible into their lovemaking.

Bucharest students Helena Fonescu and Karol Spatz were reported to their college authorities when a patrolling policeman found them making love in a public place. When details of the offence emerged the college committee decided not to suspend the couple, but invited them to help in sex education tutoring.

A couple of exuberant German tourists took a parachute ride in tow behind a speed-boat across Palma Bay, Majorca. Once in mid-air the filthy Huns performed a convincing demonstration of two aircraft refuelling in flight. The boatman, alerted by the wild cheering of crowds lining the beach, cut the tow-rope and dropped them in the sea. They swam to a raft and drank champagne until waiting policemen gave up the seige.

Traffic in New York was brought to a halt by two acrobats, Ben Flores and Isis Bermudiez, who climbed to the top of a city suspension bridge, removed their clothes and proceeded to demonstrate their agility. The New York Fire Department finally talked them down, to boos from the crowd.

York's ancient city walls are a great tourist attraction, especially at dusk when the floodlights are switched on. The biggest draw of the 1985 season was when the nightly switch was thrown to reveal a couple high on the ramparts, clearly not engrossed in an archaeological survey. Cameras clicked away at the quaint old English custom until police arrived and arrested them. They were each fined £25.

WHEN YOU SAID YOU WERE TURNED ON BY SUSPENDERS, I THOUGHT....
NEW YORK SUSPENSION BRIDGE

Reverberations

In 1980 a woman was about to take delivery of an eagerly-awaited parcel from the postman, when he snatched it back and held it to his ear. There was absolutely no mistaking the fact that it was ticking. Despite the embarrassed woman's protests the resourceful postman insisted on alerting Le Harvre's emergency services who, in turn, called out the bomb disposal squad. When she was finally able to get a word in edgeways she explained that the package contained a battery-operated vibrator which somehow had switched itself on in transit.

Strange Insurance Policies

Danish girls can insure against the possibility of being left on the shelf. Apparently many fear spending the rest of their lives as lonely spinsters, so a Copenhagen insurance company offered a policy which enables women to claim if they have not found a husband by the time they are thirty-five. And with a hefty sum under the mattress they may be happier without a husband after all.

Insurance director Kenneth Rogers is marketing a new policy against divorce. It offers special cover for the first three 'critical' years of marriage, with pay-outs spread over twenty-five years of marriage and a special silver wedding bonus. Mr Rogers, who is happily married, said: 'I thought the idea up as a joke, but people began to take it very seriously.'

Deep Throat male lead, Garard Damiano, took out a special place-of-work insurance policy in case any female co-stars became pregnant in the course of his porno movies.

Keep it up

No-one really needed the World Health Organization to announce it, but the official advice on how to live to a ripe old age is to carry on loving. Teams of WHO experts probed the inner secrets of 5,000 lovers before reaching the serious conclusion that sex is the elixir of life – a fact that millions of amateurs have known for years.

Spokesman Dr Marsden Wagner said: 'Sex is of far more value to your health than jogging or dieting. The sexually active definitely live longer and enjoy better health than those who abstain. An uncomplicated sexual relationship is good for the heart, the circulation and general well-being.' In fact just what the doctor ordered.

An Excitable Type

French writer Guy de Maupassant had a curious medical condition known as satyriasis, which displays itself in the form of a hyper-excitable penis. To say he suffered from it would be misleading. De Maupassant never regarded it as a disability – he would frequently make love half a dozen times in an hour without experiencing the slightest discomfort or exhaustion.

Robbed of His Senses

Armed raider Paul Hawes burst into a bank in Watertown, Nebraska, jabbed a gun at the nearest cashier and ordered her to hand over the money. Hawes found himself staring more at the pretty girl than the £89,000 she was nervously stuffing into his hold-all. Head-over-heels in love, he escaped and promptly rang her to apologize for his behaviour. Encouraged by waiting policemen, she chatted him up while they traced the call. By the time he had replaced the receiver he was already on his way to five years in prison.

GOODBYE
CRUEL
WORLD

Love Affairs which Ended Violently

When salesman Maurice Goldhill walked into his Detroit home and found his wife in bed with his brother, he saw red – and so did the illicit lovers. Maurice threw a whole can of scarlet paint over them before storming out.

In the grand tradition of tempestuous French affairs, Parisian Paul Cadet had a passionate row with his girl-friend and threw her from the fourth storey window of his apartment. The girl bounced off a shop awning and landed nimbly on her feet. Without any loss of momentum she raced back up four flights of stairs and promptly laid him out with a wine bottle.

New Yorker Robert Stuart decided to round off the affair with a bang when his girl-friend jilted him. He arrived on her doorstep and made his point – whatever it may have been – by sticking a 'super-blockbuster' firework in his mouth and lighting the blue touch-paper. There was a brief flash and a terrific bang. The ex-girl-friend was taken to hospital suffering from shock. Stuart is still coming down over Manhattan.

Prague housewife Vera Czermak was bitterly upset when she discovered that her husband had been having an affair with another woman. She flung herself from the third floor window of their apartment, landing on her partner and killing him outright. Mrs Czermak regained consciousness in hospital to discover that she was a widow.

Jilted husband Jack Dean decided that the only way to show how much he had suffered was to shoot himself. He drove to the house where his wife was living with another man, pointed a loaded shotgun at his head and pulled the trigger. There was a tremendous bang, but to everyone's amazement Jack was still standing there, deaf in one ear and slightly dazed. After missing from point-blank range he was treated in hospital for shock and charged with having a loaded gun in a public place.

A West German husband successfully pleaded in court that he was temporarily deranged when he strangled his wife with his bare hands. Apparently she had a habit of waking him in the middle of the night when she needed help with her crosswords.

Pulling No Punches

The *Toronto Sun* reported the story of a husband suffering from 'flu' who was attended by his local doctor. The man saw the GP kissing his wife at the door and reacted angrily. 'Under great provocation,' said his defence lawyer, 'my client almost hit him with a milk bottle, but out of respect for the doctor's profession he refrained and punched his wife instead.'

Jilted Lovers who Took on the World

Cuckolded Alfonso Monta went on the rampage through Paraguay, letting down the tyres of every parked car he could find. Alfonso, who told police that he felt deflated when his wife ran away with her driving instructor, left hundreds of motorists stranded.

Deranged American doctor Edwin Sandy spent £100,000 building a booby-trapped house of horrors to take revenge on women when his girl-friend jilted him. Invitations went out to all the women he knew for the lavish house-warming party. As they walked in the front door concealed air jets blew their skirts above the heads. As they headed for the powder-room to straighten themselves out there were baskets piled with black-face soap and cosmetic powders which turned the users' faces green.

On their return to the party the staircase suddenly straightened itself out, sending screaming girls sliding headlong to collide with incoming guests. In the bedrooms, where many retired to recover, Sandy's voice intoned warnings through hidden speakers about the unfaithfulness of women.

Those who lay down found themselves whirled from room to room as beds careered on hidden rails like a fairground ride. Downstairs, chairs and tables collapsed as diners sat down and there was hysteria in the pool when a large crocodile was seen lurking in the deep end.

Sandy was never seen in the neighbourhood again.

Suliman Kish set himself the exacting task of spitting upon the entire female population of Afghanistan. Police picked him up, still working his way through his home town, spitting on every woman he encountered in the street. Kish told magistrates that he hated all women after being rejected by a girl he had proposed to. The court told him that this was not sufficient justification for his crusade.

Acting the Goat

Pioneer transplant surgeon Dr John Brinkley is said to have become a multimillionaire in the 1930s by implanting 16,000 private male patients with goat testicles. Many were driven by anxiety that their own were wearing out after reading the doctor's persuasive advertisements. One appealing sales point was that they were allowed to choose their own goat.

Expressions for Testicles in Cockney Rhyming Slang

Orchestra stalls
Cobbler's awls
Coffee stalls
Albert halls

The Unkindest Cut of All

The Vatican used to castrate choirboys until the turn of the century to improve their singing during religious services.

Queen Semiramis of ancient Syria had the disturbing habit of ordering the testicles to be cut off her best lovers so that other women could not share the pleasure.

Vailmaila Loisi from Sydney begged her lover to give their flagging five-year relationship another chance. When Leitu Fiso refused she invited him to make love for the last time and, on impulse, cut off his penis with a knife she had been using to peel some oranges in bed. Feeling remorse, she wrapped the organ in a tissue and drove the rather shocked Mr Fiso to hospital.

'The *Sydney Morning Herald* reported that 'through the miracle of modern surgery Mr Fiso's penis was sewn back on and, according to a TV interview, was working well.' Vailmaila Loisi's solicitor said that a large number of women in the Australian community would understand her behaviour.

Roger Cox, an unemployed North Wales lorry driver who found religion, decided to remove the final barrier which prevented him from giving himself whole-heartedly to the Lord. With the help of his wife Elizabeth he studied medical textbooks, ordered through the local library, giving detailed instructions on penis amputation. Then he knelt in prayer with his wife in the kitchen of their council house and cut off the offending organ with a scalpel. Mr Cox, a father of eight, said: 'I'm happier now than I have been all my life.' Elizabeth, who travels with him, preaching from a double-decker bus, added: 'I support my husband.'

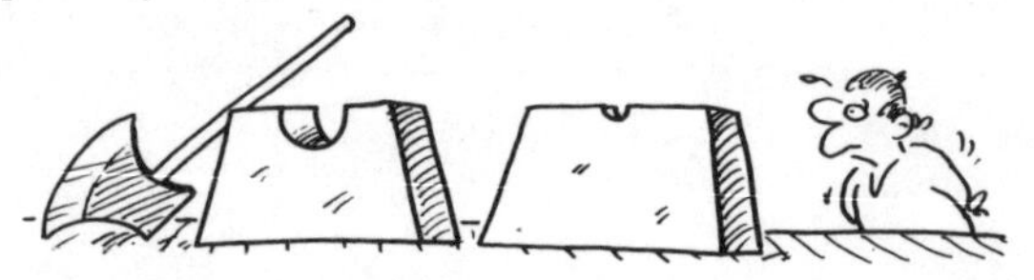

Hector Jackman was granted a divorce in Cleveland, Ohio, because of his wife's passion for writing lurid novels. The last straw, he told the judge, was when she invited local tradesmen into their home to relate their sexual experiences and made notes for her books.

Boston actress Glory Lush obtained a divorce because of a drink problem. she claimed that her husband Aubrey forced her to take off her clothes in a bar in exchange for free booze.

When Englishman Harry Dodson applied for a divorce he explained that the breakdown of his marriage had completely ruined his hobby of training snails. He was granted a decree nisi.

Benjamin Weiss and his headstrong wife Belle will be sadly missed on the Illinois party circuit. At their divorce hearing Benjamin testified that after only two drinks Belle had an uncontrollable compunction to strip off. He told the court that he had to wrestle with her before he could get her home at eight parties.

The cost of living puts a strain on many marriages – in Wilhelm Stille's case it was the cost of loving. He was granted a divorce when he told a Stuttgart court that he could no longer afford the 200 cigarettes and bottle of schnapps three times a week which his wife charged him for love sessions.

Cold showers were a passion-killer for a Swiss banker who loved them so much that he insisted that his thirty-eight-year-old wife join him for each one. Their four-year-old marriage finally vanished down the plug-hole when she was forced to endure eight showers a day. She told a Zurich divorce court: 'I was freezing like hell. I even had to take them when I was watching TV.'

A Texas woman was granted a divorce because of her husband's excessive tattooing. Not content with covering her legs in anchors, hearts and cupids, he was insisting on inscribing her back with the first verse of the 'Star Spangled Banner.'

Attilio Gianti penned passionate love letters to the married woman with whom he was having an affair, but when her angry husband sued for divorce, Attilio quickly ate his words. In the lawyer's office Attilio asked if he could have a last look at the letters. As the solicitor handed them over he stuffed them into his mouth and swallowed them. The judge dismissed the case for lack of evidence.

An English judge granted a divorce to Doris and Albert May on the grounds of irreconcilable differences when their marriage broke down after twenty-six years. Albert alleged that Doris charged him £4 each time they made love. Doris countered that Albert ran outside the house naked playing the tambourine whenever she rejected his advances.

Gene and Lynda Ballard opted for a memorable divorce in 1986 – free-fall parachuting at 120 mph (193 kmph) above California. Lynda's lawyer followed them out of the aircraft and served divorce papers on Gene at 12,000 ft (3658 m). Then, after a final mid-air kiss, Gene and Lynda dropped out of each other's lives.

When American Bruce Swain's pregnant wife was sentenced to a year in jail for drug offences, he gallantly offered to serve time in her place. After earning five months off for good behaviour, he returned home to find that she had walked out and was suing him for divorce.

In accordance with Moslem tradition an Egyptian engineer parted from his wife by intoning 'I divorce thee' three times. He made the decision after a row at Cairo airport in 1986 when she flew off to visit relatives. The engineer asked the control tower to relay the message to her plane by radio.

I'M
LEAVING
YOU
MUM
LOVE
TATTOO
TODAY

Weird Weddings

One of the world's strangest weddings took place in New York when row after row of Moonies lined up to be married by their leader the Rev Sun Myung Moon. More than 2,100 couples took their vows then pledged not to have sex for forty days. They were told instead to spend their time 'reflecting'. One point they were sure to have reflected upon was the fact that most couples hardly knew each other.

They were all matched by the sixty-two-year-old Rev Moon who was far from perfect in choosing some partners. Four brides were said to have had second thoughts, and police patrolling the ceremony dealt with reports of 'scuffles' when some of the grooms got cold feet.

At an English couple's wedding the bride looked so nervous that the vicar had to advise her to stand more comfortably to avoid fainting from the tension of the day. She relaxed a little and, without realizing, put one foot on each side of a power cable running across the aisle.

When the vicar asked the congregation if anyone objected to them marrying, there was a tremendous clap of thunder and a flash of lightning between the bride's legs. A bolt from a freak electric storm had struck the church roof, travelled down a metal ladder from the belfry and run along the power cable beneath the red carpet on which the couple were standing. Power supplies to the church were cut off and the service had to continue by candlelight.

Linda Brigett, a go-go dancer from Newport, Kentucky, obtained special permission to be married in the nude. 'After all,' she reasoned, 'I was born in the nude.' The ceremony went ahead at the night-club where she worked with the groom and bridesmaids also naked. Cameras clicked as 100 clothed guests took souvenir pictures. All insisted that the chief bridesmaid – a 45-23-39 in (114-58-100 cm) stripper – was included in the shots.

There was a colourful wedding in Cleveland, Ohio, when Violet Brown married Ray White. It hardly compares, however, with the 1963 wedding report in the *Times* which duly recorded the joining of a Mr Cock and a Miss Prick. More curiously, in 1941 a Mr Ora Jones wed a Miss Ora Jones.

Wet Weekend

The Niagara Falls, according to Oscar Wilde, were 'the second disappointment of the average American honeymoon.'

Largest Private Collection of Sex Books

The great libraries of the world all have their discreetly stored collections of sex and pornographic literature, but biographer H. Montgomery Hyde claims that the Vatican Library holds the record with 25,000 books. America's Institute for Sex Research takes second place with 20,000 volumes.

AND THIS IS THE PUNISHMENT FOR BLOWING A KISS!

Trivial Facts on Kissing

•Kissing is enjoyable, according to the *British Journal of Dermatology* , because the lips secrete a sticky substance called sebum which humans subconsciously enjoy tasting.
•On seeing an attractive woman Turkish men obtain great pleasure from kissing their own hand and holding it to their forehead.
•Kissing in public is a criminal offence in Kuwait.
•Men appear to enjoy kissing more than women. West German researchers discovered that the average male pulse rate rises to 110 when kissing; a woman's reaches 108.
•Shop assistant Michael O'Connor was taken to court for throwing his arms around a customer and kissing her on the cheek in 1907. He told Melbourne magistrates, who jailed him for a breach of the peace: 'I was in high spirits – it was a lovely spring day.'

Ten years later Michael received a solicitor's letter. The customer, Miss Hazel Moore, had died and left him £20,000 – in loving memory of the only time in her life she had been kissed by a man.
•Elizabeth Barry, of Newhaven, Sussex, gave her boyfriend a goodnight kiss – little realizing it was the last for a long time. Her jaw locked and, despite hospital treatment, stayed that way for the next six months.
•A Canadian sex researcher estimates that 97 per cent of women close their eyes while kissing, but only 37 per cent of men do.
•Drama students in Yorkshire attend a course in stage kissing. Topics range from kissing through the ages to greeting kisses and passionate kisses. The course is nearly always fully booked.
•The good news is that kissing is officially weight-reducing. One kiss uses three calories – that's 1,000 to lose 1 lb (450g). The bad news is that a group of American doctors calculated that a kiss can shorten the life-span by three minutes.

Unfortunate Double-entendres from Great Works of Literature

'He flourished his tool. The end of the lash just touched my forehead. A warm excited thrill ran through my veins, my blood seemed to give a bound, and then raced fast and hot along its channels . . .'

The Professor by Charlotte Bronte

'The organ 'gins to swell;
She's coming, she's coming! My lady comes at last.'

At The Church Gate by William Makepeace Thackeray

'"Well," said the Duchess to me, "apart from your balls, can't I be of any use to you?"'

Cities Of The Plain by Marcel Proust

'"It's just like Longueville, you know," Gordon Wright went on: "He always comes at you from behind; he's so awfully fond of suprises."'

Confidence by Henry James

'She gave a little scream, and a jerk and so relieved her-self . . .'

The Duke's Children by Anthony Trollope

'Mrs Glegg had doubtless the glossiest and crispest brown curls in her drawers . . .'

The Mill On The Floss by George Eliot

Bizarre American Dating Agencies

•*Single Animal Lovers of America*

A service for lonely hearts who want someone to love-me-love-my-pet. In the case of Shirley, a typical Hollywood client, that includes three dogs, two cats, a budgerigar, doves, a parrot, geese, chickens, one horse, a shoal of exotic fish and several wild peacocks. Understandably she advertised for a man 'with a good sense of humour'. Client ages range from twenty-one to seventy-nine, and many have entrenched domestic habits future partners are expected to adjust to. For example, one sleeps with three dogs and two cats.

•*The Celibacy Club of New York*

Women executives enrol to meet like-minded professionals who enjoy a night on the town without flirting with the opposite sex. They tour bars and night-clubs in groups of six or eight fending off sexual approaches.

•*Dull Dates of America*

This agency works on the theory that girls go for solid types with leather elbow patches who stand in a corner at parties nursing a beer all night. It was founded by Californian Joe Troise, and boasts 500 dull members worldwide, many of them English. Each carries a membership card entitling the bearer to be uninteresting without penalty or prejudice. A high proportion collect stamps, smoke pipes and wear cardigans.

•*The Atheist Dating Service*

For just $15 anyone can enrol in the hope of meeting an attractive non-believer. An initial choice of seven atheistic dates is offered, with the warning: 'Because there are so few atheists, results cannot be guaranteed.'

• *Big Gals of San Francisco*
For reasons no-one has quite fathomed, statuesque women are in great demand in San Francisco. Big Gals caters solely for overweight women looking for partners, and is astonishingly successful. A large number of enquiries have also been received from thin men, who regard big girls as 'a challenge.'

• *Fantasy of Silicon Valley*
Apart from FM radio, there was little for motorists to do, locked in the peak-hour traffic jams on the freeways of California. Then along came enterprising Barry Lorenzo with his motorists' dating agency.

When a motorist is sexually attracted to a fellow driver, he sends $5 plus his address and licence number to Fantasy who trace the owner of the car concerned and pass the message on. 'Sex flavoured with hi-tech,' is the slogan, and commuters agree that it makes driving home more interesting.

• *Tiffany Select*
This is the world's most exclusive lonely hearts club. It caters solely for millionaires who have been left on the shelf and, incredibly, there are quite a few around.

Any man enrolling has to prove he is eligible by showing the size of his bank balance. All a woman needs to qualify for registration is stunning looks. There are currently 1,000 girls on the books, but so far none of the 2,000 well-heeled agency clients has taken the plunge and popped the question.

Euphemisms No Longer in Use

Abyssinian medal – *unfastened button visible in the fly.*
To sprain one's ankle – *to be seduced.*
The apple dumpling shop – *ample breasts.*
A backgammoner – *homosexual.*
Basket-making – *intercourse.*
Brother of the gusset – *a pimp.*

Ten Common Herbs and Vegetables with Aphrodisiac Properties

Dr Paul Lee of the curiously-named Platonic Academy of Herbal Studies, in Santa Cruz, California, advocates the following herbs and vegetables to give anyone's love-life a lift. 'These natural aphrodisiacs have a potent effect on sexuality,' he claims.

Celery – a great bedtime favourite among ancient Greeks and Romans.

Ginseng – either in tea or in nourishing chicken soup for increased sexual drive.

Carrots – for maximum effect take them stewed and mixed with warm milk and honey. If you can keep that down you'll be ready for anything.

Chinese ephedra – available from health shops and said to heighten sexual awareness, boost performance and act like a charge of adrenalin.

Onions – brewed with honey and mixed with crushed chick peas are particularly effective in cold weather, says the doctor without a trace of a smile.

Saw palmetto berry – taken as a tea three times a day invigorates the body. Among the converted are a sixty-year-old impotent man who regained his sex life with a daily dosage.

Tomatoes – an effective love potion when blended with other vegetables. After all, says the doctor, they were originally called love apples.

Valerian – a natural tranquillizer which calms the nerves and improves sexual performance.

Garlic – not often recommended for making friends, but a natural stimulator, says Dr Lee, who believes that a mixture of garlic and celery juice works wonders.

Damiana – a Mexican herb said to be highly stimulating when a few drops are added to a liqueur.

Regimental Honour

After a tour of duty in Northern Ireland, forty soldiers from the Staffordshire Regiment took a holiday with their wives in Blackpool. All of them returned with an identical souvenir – the news that their wives were pregnant.

How to Catch Your Man

Mollie Meyer of Fort Lauderdale, Florida, runs a school called 'Learn to Flirt', which offers the following suggestions:

- Carry a controversial book at all times and be seen reading it in public. Ms Meyers suggests a volume called *How to Make Love To A Man*.
- Pay compliments, such as 'What a beautiful ring,' or 'I love the silver in your hair.' But, she adds, 'never more than twice in an evening – it makes your compliments cheap.'
- Hang around perfume counters, and when a man approaches spray a sample on your wrist and say: 'Could you help me out? I'd like to know if this scent smells nice to a man.' This technique is advisable only in areas where police take a relaxed view of soliciting.

Lovers' Rows about Television

Ivy Houseman, a frustrated housewife from Perth, Western Australia, was granted a divorce because her husband Willie would only have sex when the local TV station's star-gazer said the outlook was favourable.

Newly-wed Janine Sorolla was granted a divorce soon after her wedding on the grounds of her husband's 'cruel and compulsive viewing.' Janine, from Houston, Texas, even had to compete with the TV on her honeymoon. Her husband climbed into bed on their wedding night, plugged in the TV and never took his eyes from it. Even when they did make love he could not resist peeping at the screen and criticizing the actors. He carried the portable TV around the house, watching it in the bath, at the dinner table and even in the loo.

Instant Porn

A couple were arrested at Portsmouth Central Station trying to sell pornographic pictures of themselves to passers-by. They had met as total strangers only fifteen minutes earlier and hatched a plan to pose for pictures in the station photo boothe to raise money for their train fares.

Penances for Sins of the Flesh in the Middle Ages

- Nocturnal emmission – seven psalms at daybreak and dry bread and water for the rest of the day.
- Touching one's own body in a sensual manner – twenty-four psalms at daybreak.
- Masturbation – a two year penance.
- Bestiality – a two-and-a-half year penance.
- Adultery – a three year penance.
- Incest with one's mother – a three year pilgrimage.
- Homosexual act – a four year penance.
- Intercourse with a bishop – a thirteen year penance.
- Intercourse with a nun – a lifetime penance.

The Gay Rancheros

There were a high proportion of gays among Wild West cowboys, says Terri Chapman of Canada's Alberta University. Circuit judges were frequently called upon to preside over cases of 'abominable and unnatural acts.' One of the reasons, Ms Chapman claims, was a critical shortage of women: 'Cattle drives could last for months. They provided ideal conditions for homosexuality.' Wild Bill Hickock, she reveals, fell in love with outlaw John Wesley Hardin, but became disenchanted when Hardin shot a man for snoring too loud.

Male Excuses for Avoiding Sex

The marriage Guidance Council listed common bedtime excuses used by men to avoid making love to their wives:

- Bringing home work from the office and then claiming they are too tired.
- Drinking too much and saying they are tired, unwell or incapable.
- Watching late TV programmes in the hope that their partner will fall asleep.
- Engineering late-night rows to turn her thoughts away from love.
- Making the excuse that they have to go out jogging.

Full Marks for Effort

The world's largest bee, the carpenter bee, will gamely attempt to mate with virtually anything that flies. Cases have been noted of male bees trying to mate with passing birds and even light aircraft. It sounds rather grim news for hang-gliders.

Incredible Cases of Mass Swooning

Karl Hither had a way with his zither. Women in the audience at his West German concerts were known to shiver with delight. When a string broke at a particularly poignant moment during a performance in Munich, twenty-two women in the audience fainted with pleasure. Whether the cause was Hither or his zither was uncertain.

Weddings are notoriously nerve-wracking, but few match the tension of a ceremony in Chelsea when the bride was just eight minutes late. The groom, unable to take the strain, fainted, swiftly followed by the best man. The bride and her two bridesmaids arrived and promptly burst into tears. Then, when the groom recovered enough to climb unsteadily to his feet, the bride fainted.

When a handsome new foreman strode into a Texas instruments plant on his first day at work, a girl operative fainted. Before the poor fellow could recover his composure 100 other girls passed out across the factory floor. A psychologist explained that it had little to do with the foreman's good looks. Mass faintings commonly occur because of fright at the sight of someone else fainting.

In 1976 a wild rumour that oranges were causing the penises of Thai's to diminish in size caused an outbreak of mass hysteria and fainting. For weeks men could talk of nothing else. Thai women were reported to be unimpressed by the epidemic.

The Most Unexpected Virgin Birth

In 1875 the *Lancet* carried a remarkable account of an incident during the American Civil War. One of General Grant's troops was hit by a bullet which passed through his left testicle into a young nurse who was tending the wounded. The girl survived and gave birth to a baby boy, despite being pronounced *virgo intacta* by Dr L. G. Capers of Missouri.

When the baby was three weeks old the doctor was called to examine a swelling in its scrotum. An exploratory operation revealed a bullet which he deduced had fertilized the girl with semen from the soldier.

Both the girl and the trooper were told the amazing story and asked if they could meet. They eventually married and went on to have three more children, but not using the same technique.

Obscure Facts about Condoms

- French letter is probably a corruption of French bladder. Condoms made from a membrane found in sheep's intestines were once imported in great quantities across the Channel to curb the spread of VD.
- Foreigners without a good command of the language should avoid trying to buy contraceptives in Denmark. The word for them is *svangerskabsforebyggendemiddel.*
- Condoms were used by the Romans, but fell from fashion for the next 1,100 years until Italian Gabriel Fallopius reintroduced the idea. He manufactured a linen sheath impregnated with a waterproof solution.
- The word condom is thought to have originated from Dr Condom, an early pioneer of contraception, who was a doctor to Charles II.
- Goats' bladders were frequently used as condoms in ancient Crete.

Sexual Surprises Sprung on Criminals

Handbag snatcher Bill Rogers is unlikely to forget the day he picked on the wrong victim. The woman he tried to rob got the better of him and threatened to hand him over to the police . . . unless he made frequent love to her. An exhausted Rogers finally walked into an Australian police station and gave himself up.

UNDERWEAR
FOR
ANIMALS
SEXY
UNDERWEAR
FOR
ANIMALS

Widow Jasmine Blanden arrived home to find an intruder hiding in her pantry. It could have been a nasty situation, but they got around to talking and Jasmine, fifty-four, proposed an arrangement. She would feed the young man if he agreed to stay on and do odd jobs around the place. In no time at all the couple, from Canberra, Australia, were happily engaged.

The Great American Cover-up

Americans, horrified at the thought of animals walking around displaying their genitals, joined together to form the Society for Indecency to Naked Animals. The title may have lacked a certain grammatical accuracy, but zealous members all over North America descended on pets and livestock armed with a formidable wardrobe of designer clothing for animals. There were bikinis for stallions, knickers for dogs and modest petticoats for cows, but the vogue did not catch on. Farmers in particular were not enthusiastic about chasing livestock to change their underwear.

Ten Parts of a Man British Women Find Irresistible

According to a *Sunday Times* survey these are a man's sexiest attributes in order of preference:

Small buttocks	*39%*
Slim figure	*15%*
Flat stomach	*13%*
Sexy eyes	*11%*
Long legs	*6%*
Tall stature	*5%*
Hair	*5%*
Neck	*3%*
Penis	*2%*
Muscular chest and shoulders	*1%*

Ten Parts of the Body that British Men Think Women Find Irresistible

Here the *Sunday Times* found an interesting conflict of priorities.

Muscular chest and shoulders	*21%*
Big biceps	*18%*
Penis	*15%*
Tall stature	*13%*
Flat stomach	*9%*
Slim figure	*7%*
Hair	*4%*
Small buttocks	*4%*
Sexy eyes	*4%*
Long legs	*3%*

Perfect Timing

The best time for most men to have sex is first thing in the morning, according to a group of Edinburgh scientists. The body is most ready for sex soon after waking, even for shift-workers whose sexual clock adjusts accordingly.

Deadly Love

When raven-haired Yvonne Galette was caught dragging the body of her latest lover from the Bolivian village of Tambayo to a nearby swamp in 1981, the full story of her bizarre sex-life began to emerge. Police found hundreds of human bones – the remains of twenty European gold prospectors she had picked up in a local bar. After spending the night with them she killed her lovers and fed their bodies to the crocodiles.

Joe Ball, proprietor of the inappropriately-named Joe Ball's Sociable Inn, which was popular in Elmensdorf, Texas, in the 1930s, had similar tastes. Over a period of months he had sex with each of his five barmaids and butchered them before giving their remains to his pet alligators in a pool behind the inn. The crime only came to light when the mother of the final victim, Helen Brown, thought it strange that her daughter had disappeared without taking her clothes or drawing money from her bank account.

James Camb, a steward on the luxury liner Durban Castle in 1947, was charged with murdering actress Eileen Gibson. He claimed that she fell unconscious during a love session and, to avoid suspicion, he pushed her body through a port-hole.

Monsieur Gouffe, a nineteenth-century Parisian, was so infatuated with attractive Mlle Bompard that he never guessed she was planning to kill and rob him with the help of her boy-friend.

She invited the gullible Gouffe to her room and, while seducing him, teasingly slipped a silk rope around his neck. The other end was passed to the boy-friend who threw it over a beam and hauled the victim off his feet, strangling him.

Anna May Reese's husband suspected her of having an affair and set out to seek revenge. He slid a stick of dynamite beneath her mattress and ran the fuse under the floorboards and through the wall into the garden. Mr Reese waited until his wife and her lover climbed into bed and then struck a match. The couple were too busily engaged to hear the spluttering fuse racing under the floor. The explosion blew Anna May to pieces. Her boy-friend, who was lying on top of her at the time, miraculously escaped with only scorches to the palms of his hands.

Raymond de Seillans, a thirteenth-century villain, wanted to seduce an attractive woman, but her lover, Provençal poet William de Cabestan, always seemed to get in the way. So De Seillans murdered the poet and cut out his heart. He then invited the lady to a romantic dinner and served up the organ, well-cooked and decorated with vegetables. After a successful evening he revealed what he had done – more to the point, what she had eaten – and the lady fell dead on the spot.

A Shocking Business

West Yorkshire ambulance chiefs ordered the nylon carpet in one of the ambulance stations to be sprayed with water three times a week when officer Martyn Feanley made an offical complaint that his wife received static-electrical shocks whenever they kissed.

Female Creatures which Take the Initiative

The female sea horse has a strange nipple-like protrusion which she thrusts into a cavity in the male's body during mating. The female then swims off in search of other pleasures, leaving the male to carry the fertilized eggs and 'give birth' to the young.

The brain of the male praying mantis prevents him from working at his full sexual potential, so the female obligingly bites off his head during copulation to improve his performance.

The female scorpion mates tenderly and lovingly in a specially-constructed bedchamber. Then, when the act is over, she turns aggressive, kills her partner and eats him.

Breast-feeding Father

A New York father who wanted to be a good mother breast-fed his baby daughter for three months. The man, aged forty and married, achieved his ambition with a course of female sex hormone tablets, after hearing about similar experiments on animals. Gynaecologist Dr Leo Wollman, who thought the case unique, said the baby fared well under the circumstances.

Are You a Sexaholic?

Dr Patrick Carnes, who runs a therapy group for sex addicts at a hospital in Edina, Minnesota, has a working list of danger signals which denote a chronic addiction to sex.

- You promise yourself to give up sex obsessions, but always fail.
- Excessive sex makes you spend too much money and interferes with your work.
- Sexual obsessions tug at your conscience, and clash with your moral values, but you are unable to do anything about it.
- Your sex life becomes a secret which you hide from those close to you because you are afraid to talk about it.
- A preoccupation with sex interferes with your family's lifestyle.
- You exploit others for sexual needs (e.g. sexual harrassment by bosses at work).
- Sex makes you depressed, but you can do little to regulate it.
- Excessive drug-taking or drinking to enhance sexual behaviour.

The Noisiest Night of Passion

Police in Durham City surrounded a post office in 1986 to corner a gang of thieves who could be heard breaking in. But, when the law burst in they found a buck rabbit indulging his instincts with four does. 'The banging was so loud I was convinced it was burglars hammering their way into the post office,' said Mrs Mortemore, who had raised the alarm.

Rock Stars' Views on Sex

'Love is two minutes fifty-two seconds of squishing noises.' **Former 'Sex Pistol', Johnny Rotten**

'My big fantasy is to seduce a priest.' **Linda Ronstadt**

'I'm saving the bass player for Omaha.' **Janice Joplin**

'The penis is mightier than the sword.' **Screamin' Jay Hawkins**

'I've lived for years with people saying I'm a poof, but I don't give a damn. My best friends know me and that's what matters.' **Cliff Richard**

'You can't just go to bed with a cup of hot chocolate.' **John Bonham – Led Zeppelin**

All the Nice Boys Love a Sailor

Most organizations concerned with teaching the kiss of life use asexual dummies – the British Navy prefers a male. It is one of the few customers left in the world for Resusci-Andy, a

Norwegian-made inflatable male doll produced for demonstration purposes. The company's best-seller is its counterpart, the Resusci-Annie. The only other market for Andy is Moslem countries where giving the kiss of life to a female doll could be construed as offensive.

How to Spot a Sexy Lover

Writer Lailan Young, an expert in the ancient Chinese art of Siang Mien, or face-reading, gave the following tips in a 1985 lecture to the British Psychological Society.

- Tiny red dots in the eyes are a sure sign of insatiable sex drive.
- Moon-shaped eyebrows, like those of former newsreader Anna Ford, indicate a girl with a healthy sexual appetite.
- A plump chin is a sign of a high sex drive.
- Long eyelashes, like those of *Dynasty* star Linda Evans, point to a lover who is very inventive in bed.
- Anyone with small ear-lobes could be a bedroom bore with sexual hang-ups.
- If your mate has sexy characteristics – and a wide nose with a plump tip – you are in luck. It is a sign he or she will make a lot of money, says Lailan.

The Longest Love Session

Tall tales aside, this is one record which can never be accurately verified. However, there have been cases of intercourse lasting many hours. Among them was Mae West who, in her autobiography, refers to a partner known only as Ted who made love to her for fifteen hours. 'He was both astounded and pleased at his own abilities,' purred Mae.

In China mandarins would spend a day receiving callers and attending to paperwork, while still in prolonged intercourse with the same concubine.

Unfortunate Names of Real People

Major R Rectanus – former US assistant military attache.
Sharon Willfahrt – Minneapolis student.
Charles Faux-Pas Bidet – former Paris chief of police.
George Baretits – US soldier.
Ophelia Legg – resident of Norwalk, Ohio.
Luscious Pea – employee of New Orleans Charity Hospital.
Dr Fealey – gynaecologist.
Oral Love – nursing home manager.
Mr Clapp – VD centre councillor.
Needa Climax – Methodist church official.

(From a collection of remarkable names collected by John Train.)

Obscure Facts about Blushing

•Dr A.T. Harris, a biochemist specializing in human behaviour, believes that there is no way to stop a blush once it starts. 'In a sexual situation,' he says, 'It often indicates you are ready for love.'

•Patrick Pattier, a French law teacher, lost his job in 1982 because he blushingly refused to strip for a compulsory medical before a woman doctor. When he was asked to undress for the fourth successive time he turned crimson and told the doctor: 'I cannot take my clothes off in front of you, Madame.' To avoid embarrassment Patrick paid each year for a private medical with a male doctor, but his school told him that the examination did not conform to State regulations.

•If someone tells a dirty joke in mixed company it has been found that men blush more often than women.

•Mrs Brenda Selly blushed to the roots when she returned to her home in Burns, Oregon, and asked her children what they had been playing. 'Postmen,' they shouted. 'We found a bundle of old letters tied with ribbon in your dressing table

SCALPEL, SUTURE, SCAFFOLDING....

drawer, so we posted one through everyone's letter box down the street.'

•Blushing is a sign of sexual health. Endorphins, an essential part of our sexual chemistry, cause blood vessels in the face to expand in romantic situations. The effect is to make the body relax and produce a healthy, sexual glow.

The Quest for the Perfect Artificial Penis

Fifteen hundred previously flaccid Americans have derived great pleasure – at $9,000 an operation – from having Professor F Brantley Scott's hydraulic pump inserted in their penises. Applied engineering, employing the use of a small pump and cylinders, means an erection within seconds of a manual movement – and an equally rapid return to normal when the release valve is activated.

Italian surgeon Gian Franco Gabrielli advertised a £2,500 operation to improve penis size with the help of discreet internal plastic scaffolding. The doctor was jailed in 1983 when one patient complained of great pain after the forty-five minute operation.

A police spokesman in Alsace, where Gabrielli performed his surgery, said: 'Other patients seem to be too embarrassed to come forward. And frankly without them, the case won't stand up.'

Britain's National Health Service proved that it can provide support on all levels by fitting a paralysis victim with an artificial penis for the cost of only £15. Approval for the operation had to be obtained at executive level, but the result was encouraging. 'The psychological effect was fantastic,' the man's wife reported. 'It has made a new man of him.'

New techniques to surgically elongate the penis have been pioneered in Japan, where doctors have successfully grafted muscle tissue from a patient's backside to build up the tip of his penis. The result, by all accounts, is a big improvement. From the back, though, he is said to look less impressive.

Way Down Low

In 1983 *New Scientist* magizine published a survey of the love-lives of 350 opera singers. Baritones were found to have a greater sex drive than tenors because their bodies produce more male sex hormones. The magazine advised girls: 'If a man tries to pick you up, ask him to sing you *Old Man River*.'

Sexless Stories

The Irish Society for the Abolition of Sex advertised sexless package holidays in the Curragh, Ballymurphy and Croagh Patrick. A spokesman, Mr Tim O'Brien, said: 'People are fed up with so called 18-35 sun, sea and squelching holidays, and we offer an ideal alternative. Our holidays are open to anyone resolutely opposed to sex.' Life in the holiday camps was spartan, with nettle-whipping and ice-cold showers to prevent the mind wandering into squelchy areas.

In 1984 New Yorker Michael Vira, aged eighty-four, filed a divorce suit in Manhattan Supreme Court because his wife refused to have sex for fifty-four years. He alleged that Mrs Anna Vira withdrew her conjugal rights in the 1930s. At least that was his story. Anna filed a counter-claim from her home in Czechoslovakia, stating that he had waved goodbye to seek his fortune in 1926, and she heard no more of him until she received the divorce papers.

The French have always carefully nurtured their image as formidable lovers, but, according to a nationwide survey of French women, Frenchmen are not as keen on sex as they like the world to believe. Many prefer cycling or going to the cinema. After a hard working week only 17 per cent turn to thoughts of love.

Dr John Cobb, who runs a sex clinic at St George's Hospital, Oxford, says that 62 per cent of his women patients complain of a lack of interest in sex. Sexual boredom, he believes, is a phenomenon of the eighties.

An increasing number of men find that sex is a pain. Love sessions end in a blinding headache which can last for hours, Dr Edward Martin said in the medical magazine *Current Practice*. In a study of twenty-five Czechoslovakian sufferers eight men had given up sex altogether rather than run the risk of migraine.

Red Light Blues

When Moira Tan, fifty-two and 15 st (95 kg), appeared before Southwark Crown Court in 1985 charged with keeping a disorderly house, it was claimed by the prosecution that builders renovating the flat above her whipping, torture and bondage clinic had to install 4in (10cm) thick insulation to muffle the screams of clients. Miss Tan – real name Miss Bonkers – denied the charge and told the court that she was, in fact, a sex therapist and hairdresser and would have been too tired to whip clients, as the police suggested, as she had been fitted with an artificial heart valve. Indeed, she was very prudish.

Miss Bonkers, whose flat was found to contain eleven whips, four vibrators, a clamp with chains, bondage belts, eye masks, a gag on a leather strip, gas masks, plastic rope, studded gauntlets and armlets, wigs, padlocks and wooden paddles, was jailed for six months.

The Great Screen Kiss

•The first screen kiss was filmed in 1896, when audiences watched in awed fascination as actor John C. Rice locked lips with Mary Irwin in *The Kiss*. The whole reel lasted only thirty seconds.

•*Don Juan*, made by Warner Brothers in 1926 and starring John Barrymore, features no less than 191 kisses – an average of one every fifty-three seconds throughout the two-hour forty-seven-minute film.

•The longest kiss on film came in 1941 – a three-minute-five-second smooch between Jane Wyman and Regis Toomey.

•It was 1978 before the first screen kiss reached Indian cinema, and the result was national uproar. Cabinet minister M. G. Ramachandram, an actor himself, called it 'an insult', and there were mass protests in the streets.

•The first controversial gay kiss in the movies was between Peter Finch and Murrey Head in *Sunday, Bloody Sunday*. After it was shot in 1971, director John Schlesinger said that the actors were less shocked that the studio technicians. When the fuss died down, Finch was asked what his feelings were about the scene. 'I did it for England,' he replied.

•Robert Mitchum is unlikely to forget his screen embraces with Hollywood sex symbol Jane Russell: 'She's a really pleasant lady. In the kissing scenes she would pop her chewing gum up your nose . . .'

•TV's *Dynasty* cast were supplied with their own individual make-up boxes, each with its own lock and key, after Rock Hudson's torrid kissing scenes with Linda Evans, when no-one knew he was suffering from AIDS.

Stay Cool for Sex

The search for a fulfilled sex life could mean selling-up and moving house. According to worldwide statistics, the ideal temperature for rewarding sex is an all-year-round 18°C (65°F). Theoretically, any temperature above that diminishes the desire for sex; anything below and fertility is less likely.

Experts cite climatic extremes to prove their point. A prolonged heatwave in Kansas City, for instance, with temperatures in the eighties, resulted in a 30 per cent fall in the birth rate. In Montreal conceptions rise annually as the warmer summer months approach.

In general, when the temperature is above 21°C (70°F) couples are less inclined to make love. Conception is less likely below 4°C (40°F).

Bizarre Stage Acts

Hula Biggles, an exotic performer from Detroit, was banned by State authorities from playing patriotic tunes on a flute through her vagina. At her unsuccessful appeal she claimed that several mayors had praised her work, but the court declined to ask for a demonstration. Hula's abilities were, however, not as extraordinary as one might imagine. Cases have been recorded of vaginas capable of playing a harmonica, smoking a cigarette and drinking a glass of beer, though not neccessarily all at the same time.

In 1966 the liberated Danes decided to clean up some of Copenhagen's more unorthodox strip clubs. In one raid police arrested several performers, including a sixty-year-old grandmother, whose stage name was Tuppy. She told them she stripped to eke out her old age pension.

Paula Novak was a regular attraction on Sundays at the Crown Hotel, near Southampton. Her after-lunch cabaret involved strategically positioning chocolate drops over her body and inviting members of the audience to lick them off. When the case went to court, prosecuting counsel Daniel Elger QC remarked that her act 'went down like a lead balloon.'

Ploughing a Lonely Furrow

Advertisement in the *East Africa Standard*, 1975: 'Nanyuki farmer seeks lady with tractor with view to companionship and possible marriage. Send picture of tractor. Box 132, Nanyuki.'

Odd American Christian Names

Anthropologist H L Mencken noted that in the 1930s there was a vogue in the American Bible Belt for unusual Christian names. They included:

Bugger
Arson
La Urine
Dewdrop
Coita
Uretha
Cad
Blasphemy
Overy
Phalla

In the Soup

French forestry worker Gaetan le Guillou went to his doctor in 1983 complaining of dizzy spells, and was surprised when a drugs overdose was diagnosed. Madame le Guillou later admitted that she had been slipping tranquillizers in her husband's soup to curb his enthusiasm for sex.

The Body Beautiful

•The world's biggest bottoms are possessed by Hottentot women of Africa and are considered extremely attractive by Hottentot men. Cases have been recorded of buttocks measuring 3 ft (91 cm) in diameter.

•In America, where a preference for full breasts is widespread, researchers at the University of Illinois reached the conclusion that men who prefer small breasts tend to suffer from depression, or have extreme religious convictions.

•Some Victorians believed that women with a faint growth of hair on the upper lip were over-sexed.

•A herbal preparation made from the flower lady's mantle was once believed to firm-up sagging breasts.

•The world's smallest breasts are found among Mongol women of north-eastern Russia, and are considered a sign of great feminine beauty.

And Now the Results in Reverse Order

Anthropologist Desmond Morris once calculated the following vital statistics of the average woman in pre-history.

Miss Amlash 1000 BC – 38-44-78 in (97-112-198 cm).
Miss Late Bronze Age 1,500 BC – 43-42-44 in (109-107-112 cm).
Miss Indus Valley 200 BC – 45-34-63 in (114-86-160 cm).
Miss Stone Age 20,000 BC – 96-89-96 in (244-226-244 cm).

A Record Break-up

Ingrid, a housewife from Munsterland, West Germany, told a divorce court that she should have realized something was amiss when her husband Bodo took his record player on honeymoon and played 'Can't Get No Satisfaction' four times on their wedding night.

His passion for pop records in preference to Ingrid grew to a collection of 6,000 discs which filled shelves, tables and even the bathroom. 'And he carried on playing 'Satisfaction' at intimate moments when a woman does not like a musical accompaniment,' Ingrid said. 'It drove me crazy.'

When the judge granted the divorce and ordered him to pay £96 a month maintenence to their daughter, Bodo said: 'I could have bought twenty new records with that.'

Match of the Day

Claude Mercadier and his wife Josette decided to try out a new video camera by filming themselves making love, and enjoying an action replay on their TV set. They were so pleased with the results that they repeated the performance night after night. Unfortunately Claude and Josette's technical knowledge was not as good as their sex sessions. The nightly show was relayed through all the TV sets in their Nice apartment block. A fifty-four-year-old spinster, unable to watch her favourite programmes, finally called the police who arrested the Mercadiers for indecency.

The Good Nudes. . .

An interesting discovery was brought to light when a French farmer objected to nudists using a public footpath across his land. To deter them he filled his field with bulls. But, curiously, the bulls only charged people with clothes on; nudists passed safely on their way, regarded apparently, as just another animal species.

JUST SLEEPING
REST IN PEACE
RIP
I'M LOOKING UP YOUR DRESS

BRIGHAM YOUNG
Born on this spot 1801
A man of courage
And superb equipment

RICHARD KENDRICK
was buried here on
August 29th 1785
by the desire of his wife
Margaret Kendrick

Here lies the body of
SARAH
wife of John Hayes
who died 24th March 1823 AD
aged 42 years
The Lord giveth and the Lord taketh away
Blessed be the name of the Lord

ALICE MARY JOHNSON 1883-1947
Let her RIP

MARY ANNE has gone to rest
Safe at last on Abraham's breast
Which may be nuts for Mary Anne
But it's certainly rough on Abraham

In rememberance of
NICHOLAS TOKE
He married five wives whom he survived
At the age of 93 he walked to London
To seek a sixth but died before he
found her

Media Bloomers

'Jimmy Connor's wife is expecting a baby and there was some doubt about his entry. . .'

Peter West at Wimbledon

'Do you think the prisoners will regard you as a good screw?'

Jack de Manio interviewing
a new woman assistant prison governor

'A man was found wandering in the grounds claiming he was in love with Princess Anne. He was found to be mentally disturbed.'

Washington Post

'Last time out the Armagh boys accounted for Castleblayney and the wide open spaces of Omargh will suit their style of play. It promises toben aeentr fuck it to be an entertaining game, which could go either way.'

Irish News

'You have joined us at a very interesting time. Ray Illingworth is just relieving himself at the pavilion end.'

Brian Johnston

'ARCHDEACON TURNS SOD'

Headline in the Petersfield Post

'Now, are your balls high up or low down? Close your eyes a minute and dance around and look for them. Are they high up? Or are they low down? If you have found your balls toss them over your shoulder and play with them. . .'

BBC schools broadcast 1984

'The rule was that a girl would not be allowed in the bra without a man.'

Exeter Express

'There's Neil Harvey at leg slip with his legs wide apart, waiting for a tickle.'

Brian Johnston

'Aristotle Onassis, the Greek shitting tycoon. . .'

BBC news reporter

Sex-related Income Tax Claims

Appealing against excess taxation in 1984, Laslo Benkoe argued his case for a £2,000 rebate in the Swedish High Court, backed by a medical note from his doctor. Laslo was trying to claim back money he had spent on prostitutes to alleviate 'abnormally severe depression.' 'I need girls to keep my depression under some form of control,' he told Gothenburg tax office. The claim was rejected.

Lindi St Clair, nicknamed Miss Whiplash, objected to a £44,000 tax bill for her London torture chamber where she performed painful acts on wealthy men.

The Inland Revenue ruled in its wisdom that she could not claim allowances for a collection of racks, gallows, manacles, mirrors and life-size blow-up dolls. Miss St Clair complained: 'I am not being allowed a fair crack of the whip.' Faced with closing her business and seeking a more normal job, she added: 'Who would employ a woman who only knows how to pour hot wax over men, and put them in chains for living?'

Cheating, American Style

More than thirty years ago sex guru Dr Alfred Kinsey conducted a survey which found that 25 per cent of American women were cheating on their husbands. By 1983, when the

Institute for Advanced Study of Human Sexuality re-examined the problem, it was found that the figure had doubled. The most common reason for taking a lover was 'emotional dissatisfaction' with their husbands. 'Sexual dissatisfaction' took second place. More than 80 per cent said they would have liked sex more if their husbands had had better bodies. Excessive weight and pot bellies were a major source of unhappiness.

Passion Wagons

Hollywood actor Jack Lemmon's first encounter with the opposite sex was as a teenager, when he had to drink several beers to summon the courage to talk a girl into a car he had borrowed from a friend. Lemmon succeeded in losing his virginity, but not before entangling one foot in the gear lever and managing to kick a hole in the car's soft-top with the other. The excruciating pain of this uncomfortable position was misconstrued by the girl as shouts of orgasmic delight, and she whooped and screamed, redoubling her efforts as he struggled to free himself.

In 1984 Al Hamburg, of Torrington, Wyoming, sold his car to a girl in exchange for fifty sex sessions. To make the deal official Al handed her a special chart and fifty stick-on gold stars to keep a record of their transaction. But thirty-three love-sessions into the bargain – some in bed and some in the back of the car – the girl claimed that she was 'too tired' to continue. She drove away in the car and refused to hand it back. Al angrily took her to court for breach of contract. The magistrate ruled the deal illegal and allowed her to keep the car.

A Turin court heard the case against a couple who made love in a Fiat 500 bubble car in 1985. Police evidence was based on the fact that they entered the vehicle in the city centre and, within ten minutes, the windows were completely steamed up. Millions of Italians avidly followed every detail of the case – not neccessarily for its lurid content, but for clues as to how they managed the seemingly impossible.

When rescue teams were called in to free two people trapped in an Austin Healy Sprite sports car they found a semi-naked couple unable to move and in a state of great discomfort. The man had slipped a disc during intercourse. The girl, jammed beneath him, had managed to summon help by pressing the car horn with her foot.

Dr Brian Richards attending the scene in Regents Park, London, reported: 'When we opened the door the man's bare rump, trousers round his ankles, lay as if transfixed on the nude female torso. Two women volunteers had appeared to serve hot sweet tea in the best Blitz style.'

Firemen had to use cutting gear to remove the car boot and rear window to draw the couple out. As the ambulance rushed the man to hospital Dr Richards tried to comfort the distraught girl by telling her that her partner would be all right. 'Sod him,' she said. 'How am I going to explain to my husband what's happened to his car?'

Watch in Brief

Sex proceeds at a slow pace on American television, where fears of advertisers' objections are paramount. In 1984 NBC announced its sex-on-screen policy: 'Within the past year we began to allow a man to lie on top of a woman. We are reaching the point of physical motion under the covers of a bed.' The nation waits. . .

National Pride

Sexologist Dr Robert Chartham made a study of the measurements of erect penises, graded by nationality. The largest in each group were as follows:

	inches	*centimetres*
Negro	7½	19
French	7¾	20
American	7¾	20
Swedish	7¾	20
Danish	8	20.5
West German	8½	22
English	10½	27

The figures give less cause for Englishmen to boast when compared with the smallest measurements:

	inches	*centimetres*
English	2¾	7
West German	3½	9
French	3½	9
American	3½	9
Negro	4	10
Swedish	5	13
Danish	5	13

Trivial Facts about Beds

- Puppies were trained to lie motionless to act as footwarmers in draughty French beds centuries ago.
- Sleeping upright in bed was once a Norwegian tradition. Beds were made shorter because people had a fear of dying if they lay down.
- No-one in Colombia can be arrested if they are at home in bed, wearing pyjamas or night-dresses.

•A bedtime survey in New York revealed that the average Manhattan wife takes fourteen minutes to switch off the light after going to bed.
•An Indian marharajah had a bed specially made to dispense alcoholic drinks from taps concealed in wooden carvings.

The Joys of Marriage

Dr Harold Lief, director of Philadelphia's Marriage Guidance Council, reported the case of a man discharged from a New York hospital after a prolonged stay. Before he left the doctor told him that he should make a good recovery. 'But don't get too excited about sex for a while,' he cautioned. 'That's OK,' said the patient, 'I'll just make love to my wife.'

Le Pick Up

The chicest way to find a partner in Paris is to carry *la drague electronique* – a blue box emitting a radio signal which can be picked up on the boulevards by other users. It costs £90 and is about the size of a packet of Gauloises. Different wavelengths cater for heterosexuals, male gays, female gays or swopping couples. When a like-minded bleeper tuned to the same channel comes within range, both boxes emit a wailing hi-tech mating call. Parisians who like to waste no time getting to the point say it dispenses with tedious chat-up lines.

Sexy Stars of the Early Movies

Clara Bow, Hollywood's most seductive star of the 1920s, led a passionate off-screen life. She had a voracious sexual appetite which studio publicists had to work overtime to conceal. She made love to most men appearing in her movies, from famous names to extras with walk-on parts. Among her conquests, so the story goes, was the entire University of Southern California football team, which tireless Clara took in her stride.

Hedy Lamarr's first film, *Ecstasy* , was considered quite an eyebrow-raiser in its day. Director Gustav Machaty revealed years later, however, that Hedy's passionate pelvic movements were achieved by sticking a pin in her bottom during takes.

Rudolph Valentino, whose smouldering eyes caused women to swoon, was married twice. Each of his wives was lesbian and his preferences were said to be food and men, though not neccessarily in that order.

Uglies of the World Unite!

Peasant farmers of Piobbico, a hilltop village in central Italy, formed an Ugly Club 'to fight discrimination against ugly people.' The 2,000 villagers believe that they are the world's most unattractive people, and sociologists agree: 'The degeneration of facial characteristics is largely due to centuries of isolation, inbreeding and poverty,' says one expert. At a typical wedding there were cheers and applause for the bride who had cross eyes, more than a trace of a moustache, and warts on her chin.

Odd American Bye-laws

Daylight must be visible at all times between dancing couples– *Monroe, Utah.*

A man can be arrested for winking at a woman he does not know–*Ottumwa, Iowa.*

Embracing while a car is in motion is against the law–*Grand Rapids, Michigan.*

Alcoholic drinks cannot be sold to married men without the written permission of their wives–*Cold Springs, Pennsylvania.*

No person shall knowingly keep or harbour in his or her house within the city any woman of ill repute, lewd character or a common prostitute – other than a wife, mother or sister–*Ashland, Kentucky.*

If a woman berates her husband in public and a crowd gathers to listen, the husband can be fined–*Dixie, Idaho.*

Trauma in Tinseltown

Liberace, the guru of glitz, once told the story of how he lost his virginity, and apparently he still cannot decide whether or not it was rape. He found himself overpowered by a big-bosomed blues singer who slid a hand into his trousers and literally got her teeth into him. 'Then,' said the maestro, 'she crawled over my lap and screwed me. . . And oh, God! I had lipstick all over my white pants!'

It's the Thought that Counts

Greek millionaire Aristotle Onassis once spent £180,000 on a Valentine card for singer Maria Callas. It was embossed with diamonds and emeralds and, in place of an envelope, was wrapped in a black mink coat.

BUT, I ONLY ASKED YOU TO TICKLE MY IVORIES!
STEIN

Euphemisms for a Female Prostitute

B-girl (USA)
Taxi-drinker (USA)
Brass (UK)
Jane Shaw (UK rhyming slang)
Fulham Virgin (UK)
Covent Garden nun (UK)
Gentoo (South Africa)
Sister of Mercy (USA)
Pavement Princess (CB radio talk)
Thrill Dame (USA c. 1930)
Whoopie Wench (Old English)
Overnight Bag (UK)
Dutch Widow (UK)
Weekend Warrior (USA)

Australian Sexual Terms

To score between the posts – *intercourse.*
To feature with – *a euphemism for love-making heavily used by Barry McKenzie.*
She wouldn't know it if you'd been up there with an armful of chairs – *female promiscuity.*
Give the ferret a run – *intercourse.*
Spear the bearded clam – *intercourse.*
Dine at the 'Y' – *cunnilingus.*
Uncoil the pyjama python – *foreplay.*
To get off at Redfern – *coitus interruptus, a reference to the penultimate railway station before Sydney Central.*

Arresting Behaviour

The following piece appeared in the *Yorkshire Post* in 1984: 'A man found in a car with his trousers down and a woman astride him was arrested for impersonating a police officer, Leeds Magistrates were told yesterday.'

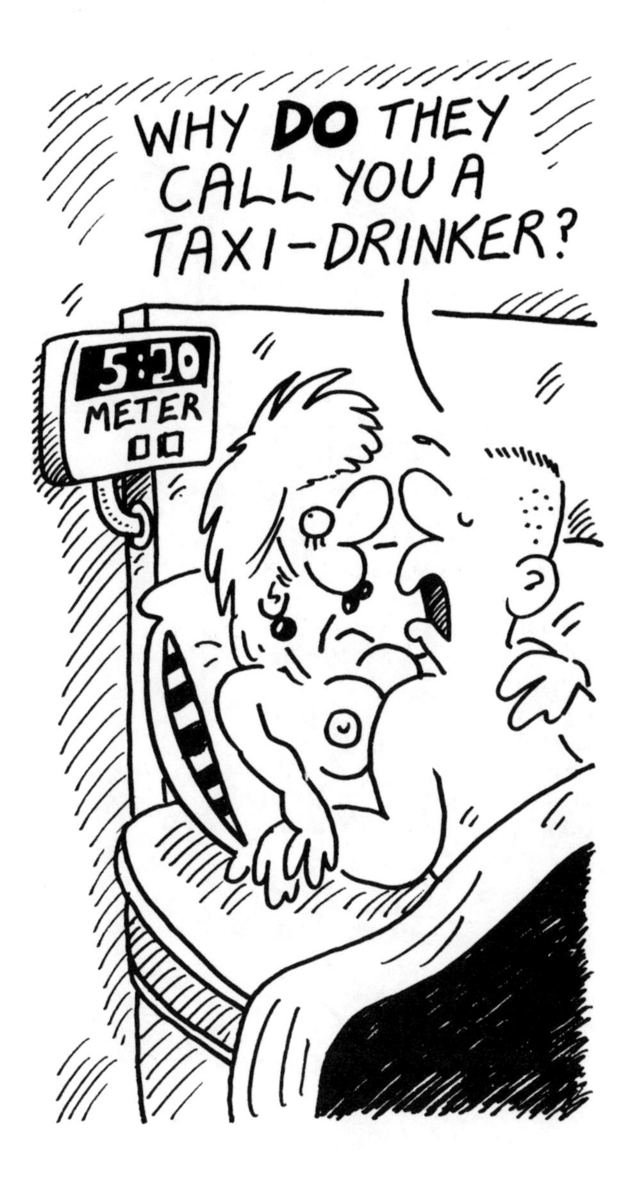
WHY DO THEY CALL YOU A TAXI-DRINKER?
5:20
METER

CINE
TONIGHT
THE KING AND I, AND I, AND I, AND....
BOX OFFICE

More People with Unfortunate Names

Ivor Krutch – Ontario taxi-driver.
Violet Organ – biographer and art historian.
Private Parts – former US Army soldier.
Joy Bang – New York actress.
Mustafa Kunt – former Turkish diplomat in Moscow.
Pensive Cocke – secretary in the US Army Air Corps.
Friendly Ley – Californian housewife accidentally shot by her husband.
Chief Unable To Fornicate – American Indian community leader.
Lettice Goedebed – Johannesburg telephone subscriber.

Slang Expressions for Masturbation in Current Usage

To bang the bishop
Meeting Mother Palm and her five Daughters
The five-finger knuckle shuffle
Hand job
A J. Arthur
A Levy and Frank
To flog the donkey
To keep the census down
Gallop the maggot

The World's Worst Contraceptives

In ancient times there was a widespread belief that charms and potions could be used to avoid conception. Among the most popular were washing the penis in vinegar, eating bees, and wearing a cat's testicles in a container around the waist.

The Husband with the Greatest Number of Wives

King Mongut of Siam, immortalized by Yul Brynner in *The King And I*, had 9,000 wives and concubines. Unsurprisingly, he died from exhaustion in 1868 while gazing at the moon.

I TRIED TO CHAT UP TOYAH WILCOX!
HEAVEN

A Final Word from the Famous

ON LUMPY TROUSERS 'Is that a gun in your pocket – or are you just pleased to see me?'

Mae West

ON WOMEN 'Women are a problem, but if you haven't already guessed, they're the kind of problem I enjoy wrestling with.'

Warren Beatty

ON WARREN BEATTY 'So we had an affair. You must be pretty bad – I can't even remember you.'

Bianca Jagger

ON MEN 'We went to a department store. There was a sign which said WET FLOOR. He did.'

Joan Rivers

ON THE JOY OF CYCLING
'I've often thought that I would like
To be a saddle on a bike. . .'

W.H. Auden

ON SEX 'I hate the whole sex scene. I'd put a bottle over the head of anybody who tried to chat me up.'

Toyah Wilcox

ON OPEN-MINDEDNESS 'I'm a practising heterosexual – but bi-sexuality immediately doubles your chances for a date on a Saturday night.'

Woody Allen

Loving is...
IMPOSSIBLE WITHOUT GENITALS